100+ IDEAS
FOR TEACHING CREATIVITY

D0533054

CONTINUUM ONE HUNDREDS SERIES

100+ IDEAS
FOR TEACHING
CREATIVITY

Stephen Bowkett

continuum

Continuum International Publishing Group

The Tower Building   80 Maiden Lane, Suite 704
11 York Road   New York
London   NY 10038
SE1 7NX

www.continuumbooks.com

British Library Cataloguing-in-Publication Data
A catalogue record for this book is available from the
British Library.

ISBN: 0826493173 (paperback)
        9780826493170

Library of Congress Cataloging-in-Publication Data
A catalog record for this book is available from the Library
of Congress.

Typeset by Ben Cracknell Studios | www.benstudios.co.uk
Printed and bound in Great Britain by Ashford Colour Press,
Gosport, Hampshire

CONTENTS

SECTION 3 **The Thinking Toolbox**

SECTION 4 Games and Activities: Visual Literacy

SECTION 5 Games and Activities: Organizing Information

SECTION 6 Games and Activities: Language and Imagination

SECTION 7   Bringing it all Together

INTRODUCTION

Ask 100 people what they mean by 'creativity' and you may well get 100 different answers. Educationally, this has been seen as a problem. Definitions (although they are not usually explanations) feel safe. Another problem, traditionally, has been the belief that creativity as an idea and as a process is rather woolly and vague, that you have to wait for 'inspiration to strike', that there are no quality controls over the outcome and that the results are not measurable in any hard or 'benchmarked' way. And yet, ironically, our modern world is filled with the wonderful products of creative thinking. The flowering of creative thought has made us what we are. And it goes on: the American business guru Peter Drucker has asserted that the currency of the twenty-first century is ideas. Employers are increasingly looking for more than just the functional skills of literacy and numeracy and a broad general knowledge.

Because of huge advances in the brain sciences over the past few decades we know more surely and in more detail that human intelligence and creativity are fundamentally linked. In terms of how we as teachers can establish a creative classroom, it's important to realize that this is not an add-on to the curriculum as it stands; rather, it's a change of emphasis and approach in how we endeavour to educate the young people who pass before us.

This book is an attempt to explain how that change may be brought about.

The Big Picture

I want to emphasize right from the start that creativity is a natural human ability. We are all born with the potential to be wonderfully creative, not just in a functional sense in order to get by in the world but, as we grow and develop, in specialized areas that capture our interest and fire up our imaginations.

There is still much false belief about creativity. Here are some of the chief myths:

o creativity is the gift of the few;
o you have to be 'bright' to be creative;
o creativity belongs to the arts and maybe the humanities, but not to the sciences – and certainly not to the world of mathematics;
o creative thinking is not disciplined, systematic, organized or logical – you have to wait for inspiration to strike;
o students need to have core skills such as literacy in place before they can be creative or original in their ideas;
o creativity is (if you want to get technical) a 'right-brained' activity;
o creative people tend to be rather eccentric;
o creative thinking skills cannot be taught.

This book is an attempt to demolish these and any other limiting beliefs about creativity that you or your students may carry. What's important is that as role models we need to do the creative attitude we want our students to have!

Activity: Ask your students about (a) what they believe being creative means and (b) what they believe being creative means in different subject areas.

Before I give you my ideas, perhaps you'd care to frame a definition for yourself. This at the very least will raise your awareness of any limiting beliefs that might still act as barriers to your thinking . . .

My opinion is that creativity is as much an attitude as it's a set of mental processes. It incorporates playfulness, curiosity, sensitivity, self-awareness and independence. It's also about making links between ideas as a habit of thought and looking at things in many different ways. If a student makes a link that he or she has never made before, then that is originality on an individual level. If a student makes a link that has never been forged before by anyone, then that idea is original on the level of humankind as a species. Similarly, a truly new perspective often leads to individual insight and illumination or, more broadly, to a breakthrough in some area of knowledge on a global scale.

The essential point is that we're all born with brains that naturally contextualize: we are 'meaning-making' beings. We are also, each of us, unique – we all have an individual perspective on the world, enriched through time by our own experience. In other words, we enter life with all the equipment we need to be creative in an increasingly powerful way. For many people, alas, this great potential is never realized and they fall back on routine thinking skills and hidebound views of the world. This is why a creative approach to teaching and learning is so vital in the twenty-first century.

Activity: Ask students to think back to a moment when they suddenly understood something new – when 'the penny dropped'. Have students explain a concept they understand to someone who doesn't yet understand it. Observe creative linking in action!

We all possess three basic mental resources. We use them anyway just to get through the day, but we can use them far more effectively as we develop our creative powers. Our resources are:

o *Memory* As we go through life we absorb huge amounts of information. We may do this formally through schooling, and certainly informally just by being alive in the world. All of this information is contextualized in our brains: it is all laid down as a kind of 'map of reality' of what we think the world is like and how each of us fits into it. That map is our memory – and let me emphasize that I am not talking about recall. Recall amounts to the strategies we have to call information back off that map in order to process it further.

o *Imagination* This is the mental ability we have to move beyond the here-and-now. For instance, I can think about what I'd like to do at the weekend. In other words, I am building a mental impression of something outside of my immediate circumstances. In other words, I've had an idea (from the Greek meaning 'mental form'). When I've based decisions on that idea, then I have 'made up my mind', which is a wonderfully descriptive phrase. To move in our heads beyond the here-and-now is an incredible power.

o *The thinking toolbox* We can do many different kinds of thinking in order to make up (or change) our minds, solve problems, form strategies, envisage goals, etc. These are the thinking tools in the mental toolbox.

Activity: Ask students, perhaps with your help, to survey some of the mental tasks they've undertaken in the past couple of days. Encourage them to consider the different *kinds* of thinking they have had to do to complete the tasks. At this stage it doesn't matter if students don't know the names of the different thinking skills, or are unable to describe them in detail. Beginning to distinguish between mental processes is a good start.

In order to use our thinking tools most effectively, we need to take account of the notion that some of them operate consciously while some do their work at a subconscious level. By this I mean that conscious thinking is thinking that:

○ we know about at the time it happens;
○ we more fully understand and can therefore explore more easily;
○ we can change by an act of will (in other words, by deliberately changing our mind).

The kinds of thinking processes that work consciously are those, for example, of reasoning, logic, analysis, discrimination, prioritization and the other so-called 'critical thinking skills'. I deal with these more fully in another book in this series, *100+ Ideas for Teaching Thinking Skills*.

Subconscious thinking goes on largely 'behind the scenes'. In other words, we're mentally processing things but don't realize we're doing it. So, the dreaming we do at night is subconscious. We are largely unaware of dream content (two to three hours each night), although we may remember fragments and can, in fact, train ourselves to have greater dream awareness.

We are subconsciously busy in the day too, as when we struggle for a while to recall someone's name, only to give up the effort and say 'Oh, it'll come to me.' Often, later, it does, and that is the result of subconscious work that went on in the meantime.

In order to develop fully our students' (and our own) creative powers, it's necessary to use both conscious and subconscious tools in combination to achieve the desired outcome.

Activity: Give your students an obviously conscious mental task to do, like remembering a list or putting the items in the list in a certain order. Now ask them to begin telling you the route from school to home. Point out to them how, in this second case, images and understanding rise effortlessly and spontaneously from the subconscious.

THINKING WITH THE WHOLE MIND

The neocortex is the most recently evolved part of the human brain. It is divided into the left and right cerebral hemispheres, joined by a bridge of nerve fibres known as the corpus callosum. Crudely put, the activity of these hemispheres corresponds to conscious-critical and subconscious-creative thinking processes: in some educational literature the left and right hemispheres are called the 'logic brain' and the 'artist brain' respectively.

Because subconscious thinking tools operate largely outside the realm of conscious awareness, they are often not used deliberately or, in some cases, even recognized as being central to the whole development of creativity. Where such 'hidden workings' are factored in, they tend to be shrouded in mystery. This, I think, is where we get the vague and unhelpful language of the creative process, such as 'waiting for inspiration to strike' or 'my Muse has deserted me', or 'it's no use, my creative energy is completely blocked today'. Such ideas, supported by the platform of false belief, inhibit the systematic use of creative thinking tools.

The fact that subconscious processing goes on without us realizing it does not and should not hinder creative development. We don't need to understand something completely in order to use it effectively. What we can easily do is, by noticing outcomes, deduce and intuit underlying mechanisms and principles. And before we notice outcomes, we can notice the subtleties of the way we feel as thoughts occur that clue us in to the fact that the 'right brain' is contributing to the life and success of the whole individual.

Activity: Ask students to look at dot-to-dot pictures and notice how, very often, they can see the patterns immediately. Then prepare a sheet covered randomly in dots. Give groups of students different categories to look for: machines, animals, letters, constellations, etc. These tasks highlight the pattern-recognition abilities of the right cerebral hemisphere.

- The adult brain weighs about 1.3 kilos, the same as one and a half bags of flour.
- Your brain weighs about 2 per cent of your body, but uses around 20 per cent of your energy.
- Brain tissue is folded up in a very complex way, to pack lots of surface area into a small space.
- Messages from the brain travel to all parts of the body at 650 feet per second.
- The brain is made of one hundred billion (100,000,000,000) cells called neurons.
- Each brain-cell branches like a tree. Electrical and chemical messages constantly pass from cell to cell – this is the thinking we do.
- Human consciousness may be different from that of other conscious creatures. Cats, for instance, are aware: clearly they are conscious. But people *are aware of being aware*, which essentially allows us to think about our thinking and choose from a selection of thinking 'tools' depending upon the mental job we have to do.
- As we think, we lay down neural pathways in the brain. We can deliberately create new pathways and establish positive and powerful habits of thought.
- We are all naturally creative. Our brains love to connect, explore, make patterns, imitate and innovate, engage in a diversity of experiences and rise to new challenges.

Activity: Ask students to research another piece of gee whizz information about the brain.

GEE WHIZZ FACTS ABOUT THE BRAIN

Our various mental states (listed below) are reflected in the differing frequencies of electrical impulses produced by the brain. We have all experienced them and do so many times each day. But again, with some training we can learn to 'shift state' at will, depending on the kind of thinking we want to do.

○ *The beta state* is characterized by the brain producing electrical impulses of around 13 to 25 cycles per second (cps). This is the state of conscious alertness when our point of attention is fixed more on the outside world and our critical thinking skills are engaged. When, as teachers, we ask children to give us their undivided attention and think carefully about what we say, we put them in beta state (apart from the ones who are staring out of the window!).

○ *The alpha state* is around 8 to 12 cps. This is the powerful learning state of 'relaxed alertness', when our attention is divided between what's happening in the outside world and the thoughts we are having about it. In other words, we are aware of our own conscious 'meaning-making' at that point: we are noticing our own systematic daydreams based upon what we are hearing, seeing, etc.

○ *The theta state* is around 4 to 7 cps. This has been called the state of deep reverie. Here we are intensely absorbed in our daydreams, which may have the quality of dream imagery as information rises from the subconscious part of the mind. In theta we lose ourselves in thoughts, the significance of which may only become apparent later.

○ *The delta state* is around 0.5 to 3 cps. This is dreamless sleep when consciousness is absent.

Activity: Ask students to keep a diary of their mental states over a day or two. Encourage them to notice what can affect those states: for example, mood, time of day, eating a meal, etc.

A creative attitude should underpin the acquisition of the core skills, such as literacy and numeracy. An attitude is by definition a 'fixed position', but ironically, when we take a creative attitude to life, we're always prepared to look at problems from many angles. We make links between conventionally separate or previously unconnected ideas. We delight in the unexpected, we relish thinking challenges and we realize that to have good ideas we need to have lots of ideas. In other words, we enjoy thinking and playing with information.

When I talk to students about having a creative attitude I tell them that to get lots of good ideas, they need to be nosy, which they generally appreciate because they already are! I go on to explain that we can be nosy in two very important ways – by noticing things and by asking questions.

Furthermore, we can notice things going on around us, and we can notice things going on inside our own heads. It is widely recognized that students' learning develops more quickly when they practise *metacognition*, which means thinking about the thinking you do. In order to achieve that, of course, you must first notice what's going on in your mind.

And being nosy by asking questions leads to a deeper understanding of different kinds of questions; whether they are scientific/technical, philosophical, small or large scale, open or closed, etc. To have this degree of awareness leads towards 'quality questioning'.

In a nutshell, to be creative you need to be nosy!

Activity: Ask students to notice something in the classroom that they've never noticed before. Deliberately place something new in the classroom every few days. Invite students to ask a question about something that truly puzzles and intrigues them. You may not know the answer – so invite students to come up with effective ways of finding out!

MANY VIEWPOINTS

The ability to look at things from a range of perspectives is a valuable skill in developing creative thinking. It comes down to mental flexibility. This allows us to apply and further appreciate the Principle of Potential (see Idea 33).

The 'many perspectives' aspect of the creative attitude allows students to 'handle information ' (see Idea 10) flexibly and adventurously. It also embodies and encourages strategic thinking, which always allows for many possible routes to the solution of a problem.

In terms of dealing with other people, we can bear in mind the insight of the writer Anaïs Nin that 'We see the world not as it is, but as we are.' Two immediate and powerful implications of this are that we can change the way we are at many levels and we also have the creative ability to see the world from another person's point of view, which is the essence of empathy. Empathy of course requires that we actively seek to *understand* another person's viewpoint: simply to weep as someone else weeps is, strictly speaking, sympathy, which involves feelings but not necessarily the leap of imagination into the other person's world that I am talking about.

We can take the notion of 'many viewpoints' further. A valuable insight and a working rule of the creative attitude is that to have good ideas we need to have lots of ideas. Furthermore, even ideas that don't seem that good to begin with can, if looked at differently, become more useful, appropriate or powerful.

Activity: Review past lessons or preview future ones and consider how else they might be structured to further develop your students' creativity.

It is now widely recognized in the educational world that traditional definitions and supposed measurements of intelligence have been very limiting and grossly underestimate the power and diversity of the human mind. Intelligence is still often associated only with 'academic ability', which places more emphasis on conscious critical-thinking skills and the retention and recollection of facts under formalized conditions.

If we are prepared to consider, however, that intelligence is our general ability to handle information, then this new, looser definition incorporates whole-mind thinking including the subconscious processing that goes on behind the scenes. We can now build notions of creativity into what it means to be intelligent, and intelligence into ideas of what creativity involves.

Another dimension of what intelligence means is to be found in the work of the American psychologist Howard Gardner. Gardner's famous *multiple intelligences model* suggests that we handle information across a range of naturally occurring areas or domains of knowledge and understanding.

If I am curious about numbers and I notice how numbers interact and form different combinations which have applications in the world, and if I'm happy to play with numbers and explore them and be curious about them, then my 'numerical intelligence' will develop more quickly.

Similarly, if I'm nosy about words and I notice how the written and spoken word affects my thoughts and feelings and may change my outlook on life, and if I play with language with the intention of turning it into a life-transforming tool, then that creative attitude to words will naturally allow my 'linguistic intelligence' to flourish.

Refer to Gardner's works to appreciate the richness and elegance of his ideas, but at this point let's keep in mind that creativity and 'the intelligences' develop hand-in-hand.

Activity: Ask students to consider a topic, subject, hobby, etc. that they understand very well. How do they know they understand it, as opposed to simply knowing a lot about it? Ask students to notice how they *feel* as they talk about something they understand well.

UNDERSTANDING OR 'UNDERSTANDINGS'

Consider what 'understanding' means. For me it's more than just knowing. To understand something implies experience, familiarity, confidence, independence of judgement – in fact many of the qualities we find in the creative attitude itself. Understanding an area of knowledge opens up the opportunity to play creatively in that arena.

Professor Kieran Egan has done for understanding what Howard Gardner did for intelligence by suggesting we evolve through a hierarchy of understandings as we grow and develop.

Newborns and young babies have a *somatic* understanding of the world, whereby the meanings they make are referenced through bodily sensations. They are warm or cold, hungry or thirsty, comfortable or uncomfortable. Slightly older children still live in a world full of wonder and mystery, and with their growing mental capabilities develop a *mythic* understanding: they make sense of what's going on by making up stories and mythologizing.

Beyond this stage, children from the ages of around 7 to 11 display a *romantic* understanding, in the sense that they still regard the world with wonder, but are actively seeking limits and boundaries to what is known. They want to put a border around reality. Increasingly, this conceptualization is framed in language, leading to an adult *philosophical* understanding of things whereby the meanings we make are generally expressed in words.

However, if this were the epitome of human understanding it's easy to see how people might be limited by their own linguistic frameworks, leading to mindsets ('minds set') that do not admit the unconventional, new, strange or apparently inexplicable. Kieran Egan suggests that we grow beyond philosophical understanding into an *ironic* understanding of reality, whereby we can examine, question, doubt and reconstruct our frameworks in a spirit of curiosity, playfulness and experience; this is a creative attitude.

Activity: Ask students to think back to some earlier belief or understanding. For example, how thunder occurs, or why the sun rises and sets. Explore with them how they came to that understanding. Were they simply told? Did they make up a story to explain the mystery?

We cannot help but practise 'meaning-making' (to use a phrase coined by Marshall McLuhan): we need to make sense of the world in order to survive. As I've suggested, much of this processing goes on subconsciously, a phenomenon recognized long ago by the mathematician Henri Poincaré, who identified what have come to be known as the four classical steps of the creative process.

○ *Preparation* Absorbing information gives us the raw material to be creative with! We might absorb this formally through schooling, and certainly we absorb huge amounts of information simply by being alive. How we engage with it counts – as the saying goes, 'discovery favours the prepared mind'.

○ *Assimilation* This is the putting together of what the world means to us, the making sense of the raw stuff of experience – the in-forming of the map of reality. In terms of our interests and creative goals, many people focus their creative energies into quite narrow areas of study, so their insights and creative breakthroughs happen in that particular field.

○ *Illumination* The light goes on, the penny drops, we have a 'Eureka moment'. This is the point of insight when we make a leap of understanding. At this moment we recognize a previously unknown link or see the world in a way that's new for us. Illuminations form the fruit of the creative tree which has its roots in childhood play and the joy of exploration.

○ *Verification* Having learned from within, we need to test our insights against outside reality. The best ideas work for everyone.

Activity: Ask students to list the ways in which they absorb information, then range these along a line from 'informal' to 'formal' – so having a casual conversation with someone is a more informal type of *preparation* than asking that person considered questions.

Activity: Tell your students that you'll be giving them some new ideas about a certain topic in a day or two. Suggest also that in the meantime they'll notice previously learned ideas on the same (or similar) topic popping into their minds. Ask them to jot these down.

13

From what I've said so far you can probably work out what limits and inhibits the creative process. I've found the following to be a useful checklist:

o a fear of making mistakes, giving the wrong answer, appearing foolish;
o a fear of change;
o a fear of consequences;
o unchallenged habits of thinking;
o unchallenged frameworks of language;
o unchallenged principles and previous models of understanding;
o unquestioning acceptance of 'absolute truths';
o attachment to the familiar and comfortable (in terms of beliefs, etc. – it's OK to hang on to your favourite sofa);
o solid certainty;
o ongoing self-doubt and negative self-judgements;
o over-reliance on rational thought, outside authority and expertise;
o unwillingness to explore, experiment and play.

Activity: Ask your students to be honest in thinking about which of the above points affects their learning. (Adapt the vocabulary as necessary to suit the age of the students.)

Many of the blocks to creativity give rise to what has been called 'reactive' thinking. Reactive in the sense that such thoughts remain unexplored, unquestioned and unchallenged – we are reactive rather than proactive in the way we make sense of the world. Such an environment is characterized by:

o the frequent asking of closed and/or rhetorical questions by the teacher;
o the simple restatement of 'facts' by both teacher and pupils;
o 'grasping and telling' behaviour in children – where pupils use the 'right answer' they have been told as a security and protection – such a reaction usually conceals a fear of being wrong;
o by extension, right answers are presupposed and a world-picture has been predefined (without input from or negotiation by pupils);
o reactive thinkers rely heavily on outside authority and 'preprocessed' content;
o reactive thinking flourishes in an environment where content is covered (rather than ideas being uncovered and discovered);
o reactive thinking usually occurs where the teaching–learning ethos is judgemental, competitive and hierarchical;
o such an ethos (re)actively inhibits most, or all, of the aspects of creative thinking.

When I talk of such things I am often challenged on the point that 'right answers' actually exist, and besides there would not be time for children to rediscover the wheel for themselves in every case. This is true, of course, and what I'm suggesting is a matter of balance; the establishment of an environment wherein as teachers we can cultivate a creative attitude.

Activity for the teacher: Consider doing a reactive thinking audit of your teaching style. How many of the above points, and to what extent, apply to your current approach?

IDEA

15

THE CREATIVE ENVIRONMENT

Having looked at the 'reactive environment', by contrast the creative classroom:

○ is organized and ordered, yet there is the flexibility to generate ideas within the structure of teaching and learning the curriculum;

○ focuses thinking and energy through precise, but often open-ended, tasks which have as a fixed goal the real development of understanding;

○ cultivates a climate where creative thinking flourishes constantly but keeps the threat (of feeling foolish, etc.) low;

○ encourages high expectations in children and presupposes them in teachers;

○ reflects on the use and appropriateness of value-judgements;

○ encourages self-evaluation (for example through the 'critic phase' of the Disney Strategy in Idea 18) and cultivates self-esteem;

○ considers problems as learning opportunities;

○ encourages the flexible use of many kinds of thinking tools towards the goal of children being 'high-order' (creative and powerful) thinkers;

○ exploits the 'principle of utilization' whereby teachers use what the students bring into the classroom and feed it back as positively as possible;

○ makes fun a central component of the teaching/ learning process.

Activity for the teacher: If you feel you don't already build some of the above aspects into your approach, select one or two you feel comfortable with and consider in detail how you can apply them.

Activity for the students: Ask students to discuss previous lessons they remember well and that made a positive impact. Try to get some consensus about what makes a great lesson. List these aspects and set them against the suggested framework for a creative environment.

THE PYGMALION EFFECT

In 1968 Professor Robert Rosenthal published a book called *Pygmalion in the Classroom,* in which he explored the implications of research into teachers' expectations of students' performance. Basically put, if teachers expected students to perform well, they did. And if teachers expected students to perform less well, they did that too! Rosenthal's work in this field has been extensive and the basic premise stated above, which has come to be known as the Pygmalion Effect, has been verified time and time again across the age and ability range.

One the best-known pieces of research in the field was carried out at a school called Oak Hill. Here, teachers were encouraged to believe that certain students (selected at random for the experiment) were showing signs of a 'spurt in intellectual development'. By the end of the year, exposed as they had been to their teachers' expectations of improvement, the experimental group showed significantly greater gains in intellectual growth than comparable students in a control group. For example, first-graders in the control group displayed a gain of twelve IQ points, while their contemporaries in the experimental group showed a 27.4-point jump in IQ. Overall across the age range of the experiment, students in the experimental groups showed an almost four-point gain in IQ, which is still statistically significant.

What we have here of course is the phenomenon of the self-fulfilling prophecy. Professor Rosenthal and other researchers have been at pains to point out, however, that while some educators might feel that this is all a matter of common sense, teachers' expectations are sometimes not obvious even to the teachers themselves, and are communicated non-verbally in many subtle ways.

Suggestion: As we develop the creative attitude in our students, then, perhaps we need to explore the sincerity of our own beliefs that

o all students are creative;
o all students can be enthused.

THE CREATIVE CONTRACT

Establishing the creative classroom is a collaborative act between teacher and students and, beyond that, works more powerfully when it's built into the educational ethos of the whole school. If all staff and pupils are prepared to buy into this approach and make a commitment towards it, creativity will quickly underpin all that goes on within the school.

Many of the points listed in the previous ideas form the creative contract which consolidates the values underpinning the teaching and learning process. Further aspects of such an agreement are:

o encouraging *active* noticing and quality questioning;
o making thinking explicit – noticing students' language and use this to raise awareness of what has gone on in their heads to produce that spoken or written response;
o using thinking tools for both analysis and synthesis (to deconstruct other people's ideas and to generate your own) across the curriculum;
o establishing the principle that whatever students put into their work should be there for a good reason;
o making it clear that all ideas are valuable;
o encouraging individual responsibility within a climate of mutual respect (initially for others' ideas, but more generally as one human being to another);
o realizing that 'what's known stays known' – as the old saying goes, 'Three things cannot be taken back: time, the arrow in flight and the spoken word.'

Activity: Discuss these ideas with your students and draw up a creative contract poster. Encourage students to 'buy into' the contract. Give sincere praise when they do.

Building the Creative Environment

DO IT LIKE WALT

Walt Disney was undeniably a highly entrepreneurial, successful and creative individual. Friends and colleagues noticed that when he was developing his projects he would go through different phases of thinking, which corresponded with different mental states (see also Idea 7). These 'thinking moods' in turn reflected the use of various thinking tools.

At the outset Walt Disney would give himself some daydreaming time as he allowed the 'grand vision' to rise up from the subconscious. 'What if I could build a city like something out of fairyland and people it with characters from my movies? And what if people came from all over the world to talk with Donald and Mickey?' This is the so-called 'dreamer phase', an uncritical exploration of the big idea.

In order to realize the vision Walt Disney would need to plan. This requires holding on to the broad context of the dream, but using more conscious analytical thinking tools to actualize it in the world. The 'realist phase' endeavours to answer the question 'how can this be achieved?'

Finally, when the plan had been created, Walt Disney would detach himself from the dream, look back and ask 'what changes do I need to make for this to be the best plan I can make?' The 'critic phase' reviews the work through a more (constructively) critical eye.

This way of approaching problems, by developing opportunities and achieving goals through thinking, doing and reviewing, has come to be known as the Disney Strategy. Pupils' learning might well develop more powerfully when they 'do it like Walt'.

Activity: Decide on a project and have students deliberately model the Disney Strategy. One example is an adventure holiday. Students first envisage where they'd like to go and what they'd like to do. Encourage systematic daydreaming. Then have them plan the itinerary. When that's done, ask students to review the plan with the intention of, for instance, making it more cost- or time-effective, more enjoyable, more inclusive for all students, etc.

These two kinds of thinking are useful in many ways in establishing a creative classroom. The point to remember about goals is that they are fixed. Our primary aim as teachers is to help our students become independent, creative individuals empowered to carve out for themselves fulfilling and successful lives. That is the point towards which all of our endeavours are aimed. In order to achieve that, we must consider many smaller goals, down to the level of the minutiae of the lessons we plan.

Strategic thinking is the 'how' that enables goals to be achieved. Strategies are 'ways of doing' and are, and should always be, amenable to change. Strategies, then, are constructed from tasks that are the building-blocks to learning. If any particular strategy fails to work for a given student, then instead of doing that strategy 'longer, harder, louder', we are bound to dismantle it and build another more effective one. For me this goes to the heart of differentiation.

Activity: Using the adventure-holiday example in Idea 18, discuss with your students the various sub-goals that make up the overall aim of 'having fun seeing the world'. Now introduce problems (e.g. an airline strike) and invite students to come up with alternative strategies that still allow them to attain their goal.

GOAL-ORIENTED AND STRATEGIC THINKING

PROACTIVE VERSUS WISHFUL THINKING

The use of strategies to achieve goals involves proactive thinking, which means 'acting in advance to deal with expected difficulties'. In other words, thinking about problems that might lie ahead. Although the dreamer phase of the Disney Strategy encourages letting the mind wander within a certain area of interest, this isn't passive or wishful thinking. Let me clarify what I mean.

Proactive/goal-oriented thinking

o is under the individual's control, even when it involves subconscious processing;
o involves a clear sense of direction and destination;
o necessitates planning and review at each stage;
o flourishes in the presence of excitement and curiosity;
o recognizes strategies as processes focused on fixed goals;
o verifies and validates ideas and solutions externally *and* by using 'internal referents' (one's own thoughts and feelings as a basis for sound judgement);
o expands and diversifies, while exploiting all available resources;
o remains rational and realistic, even while using what may appear to be irrational subconscious abilities and fantasy as a metaphor within the thinking arena;
o supports and is supported by self-belief, is strengthened by commitment and driven by joy.

In many ways, wishful thinking is the opposite of the items in this list. It is passive and uncontrolled – we let our imaginations run away with us. It involves hope rather than intent and remains fixated on an end-point rather than valuing the processes and strategies that would bring the end-point within reach. Wishful thinking tends to be internal and disconnected from outside reality. It is often simply and wildly fantastical and unsupported by self-belief or any commitment.

I bear this in mind every time I'm tempted to buy a lottery ticket.

Activity: Ask students to come up with examples of things that are wished for. Draw up a general wish-list. Now discuss ways of achieving those goals, anticipating possible problems that might occur.

To encourage means 'to give courage to', which takes us right back to the central idea that effective, creative thinking is fundamentally bound up with one's emotional outlook, self-confidence and self-esteem. When we work to develop our students as creative thinkers we are working within the field of emotional resourcefulness. Most of the activities I explore in this book develop confidence and thinking in tandem – the 'creative attitude' is as much an emotional stance as it is a mental one.

As teachers we can best encourage our student's creativity by being creative ourselves. We are powerful role-models: when we take a creative approach we verify for the students that it's OK for *them* to be like that. However, there are particular things we can say to students which make our encouragement explicit. An encouraging teacher might say:

O That's a good idea. How can we build on it? Where can we take it from here?
O Tell me more about this. What steps did you take that led you to this point?
O What other solutions will you go on to find now?
O What further options occur to you now? Of course you can decide which one to take.
O If this were an opportunity rather than a problem, what would you do now?
O What other approach will solve this problem, do you think?
O How would [choose a person, cartoon character, comic book hero, etc.] deal with this, do you think?

Let older students spend some time with a class of younger learners, using the language of encouragement given above.

Activity: Ask younger students to make 'encouraging language stickers' (adapting the vocabulary as appropriate) which they wear for the day. They will act as visual reminders of how to comment positively on each others' ideas.

ENCOURAGING CREATIVITY

The 'map of reality' that I've already referred to has also been called the *thoughtscape*, the mental landscape of memory upon which we draw, consciously and subconsciously, in order to make sense of the world. Representing (re-presenting) the world in the imagination can change the way information is encoded on the memory map. Thoughts have their physical analogue in the brain in the form of neural pathways – electrochemical connections between brain-cells or neurons. In other words, thinking creates and establishes neural networks, which collectively might be referred to as the *brainscape*. The detail of the hardwiring is down to our experience and what we make of that experience.

We are born with our brains already hardwired with the potential to learn language. Language is fundamental to the way in which we process information. Words influence our perceptions increasingly as we grow. In one sense we are very much what we say, and how we interpret what is said to us.

The world of words that mirrors the world of our experience is our *wordscape*. Passively accepting the wordscape at any point leads to a 'hardening of the categories', a freezing of the metaphors through which our experience is filtered. Constantly engaging and playing with language and exploring the wordscape helps us develop a creative attitude and make us more powerful thinkers.

Activity: Notice how your language 'frames' your world. Become more aware of generalizations, negative thinking and assumptions, for instance. When you become more aware of these things in your own language, raise your students' awareness of their limiting language. Help students to reframe unhelpful metaphors, such as:

○ I can't imagine myself doing that. (Pretend you can and tell me when you've done it.)
○ I've never been any good at maths. (What exactly stops you from improving now?)
○ It's all the same in the end. (What precisely is 'it'? *All* the same? Explain more about what you mean by 'the end'.)

'The word is not the thing.' The map is not the territory. The wordscape by which we express our understanding is, in essence, a metaphor. Language is always representational. On one level, the language of a school subject is merely a way of looking at the world, a lens if you like. As a scientist I look at the world through a scientific eye. As a historian my perceptions are filtered through my experience and expertise in that subject. A poet and a mathematician can gaze at the same view and see very different things.

An immediate and vital implication of all this is that in teaching a subject we're encouraging our students into new ways of looking. They will tend to express their perceptions through the vocabulary of specific subject areas. It has been said that any subject boils down to its vocabulary: the essence of understanding the world biologically, geographically, historically, etc., is established, tested, verified or challenged through the words of these subjects as they are used by the students.

The point I want to make clear is that each word and sentence is a metaphor, which builds into larger and more overarching metaphors representing our collective understanding of any subject as it relates to the 'real world'. Helping our students to become linguistically intelligent across the subject range feeds their creative attitude, which in turn supports their growing understanding.

Activity: Examine everyday metaphors with your students. Look at phrases like 'It's an uphill struggle', 'I'm feeling on top of the world', 'I've got my head in the clouds', etc. Raise their awareness of how common and diverse metaphors are in our language.

As part of my own creative attitude I came to realize the importance of certain words and how they have helped to develop my thinking. I list some of them now by way of summing up points I have already made, and as a precursor of what is to follow.

○ *Idea* Linked to 'I see' and 'to know'. Also 'a mental form'. For me the phrases 'making up your mind' and 'changing your mind' are important and telling. Doing these things effectively is a mental skill.

○ *Insight* As I often say to students, we need to look in to find something out. Our insights help to determine our outlook on life. An 'inlook' therefore is valuable!

○ *Intuition* I think of this as 'inner tuition'; thoughts and feelings (which are internal resources and self-referents) that help us to feel secure and independent in our judgement.

○ *Lesson* Rooted in 'to read', it has links with 'legend', which I define as a marvellous story – and want to think of my lessons that way.

○ *Recall* To call information from the map of reality in order to do something with it in cognitive space. To recall is not exactly the same as to remember, which means 'to bring back again to the members' – to recreate in the flesh the emotions and sensations present at the time of the first experience. Lessons, therefore, should be positively remembered.

○ *Recognize* To 're-cognize' is to bring ideas back into cognitive space. For me recognition means that these ideas are ones that I've consciously worked on before.

Activity: Explore with your students simple links between words. Delve into etymology where appropriate. Look, for instance, at author and authority; emotion, motive and move; creative and creature, etc. Draw out from the students how the words and the ideas they represent have important things in common.

Metacognition has been defined as 'thinking about the thinking you do'. To do that we need to notice the thinking that we're doing in the first place. Being in alpha state (see Idea 7) heightens self-awareness of what is happening in cognitive space: noticing thinking simply requires a slight turning inward of the attention so that we're balanced between being completely focused on the outside world and being totally lost in a daydream.

Even when we notice these transient and ephemeral ideas, to be competently metacognitive we also need to take into account the following.

○ *The speed of thought* Ideas can happen quickly. Part of our students' metacognitive skill is in their realizing that the mind works fast and that any fleeting notion or inkling is valuable.

○ *Irrationality* Creative ideas often come in at an angle. Insights might seem crazy or bizarre, but valuing them and accepting they might well make more sense later is part of a creative attitude.

○ *Ambiguity* A creative idea might not be *an* answer but *many* answers, perhaps some of them to questions that we have not yet posed, or solutions to problems that have not yet been consciously recognized.

○ *Symbolism* By the same token, an idea might not seem to be literally true or, apparently, logically complete. Because the language of the subconscious is that of metaphor and symbol, an idea will often be the tip of the iceberg.

All of these facets of metacognition imply faith in, and reliance upon, the subconscious as a resource.

Activity: Play a game of 'what do you get if you cross A with B?' Try crossing a house with a car, a torch with a walking-stick, a hat with a TV, a pencil with a mobile phone, etc. It's likely that most students will almost *instantly* create an impression of such things in their minds. Reinforce the notion that ideas which seem illogical or impractical at the outset might well develop into useful new inventions.

METACOGNITION AND CREATIVITY

FINDING A BALANCE

A creative classroom is one where continual adjustments are made to find a balance between:

○ teacher talk – class and group discussion;
○ pupils listening to acquire knowledge and instruction – interacting with information;
○ group work – teamwork;
○ routine functional questions – quality questioning (see idea 89);
○ being told – finding out;
○ receiving explanations – rediscovering the wheel;
○ giving the 'right answers' – (re)solving problems;
○ using critical/analytical thinking to focus down – using creative thinking to speculate and expand;
○ copying/reproducing ideas – inventing;
○ describing – visualizing;
○ paper-based exercises – real-life challenges.

Activity: Carry out an informal audit to check the balance in your classroom.

'SOBs' are Specific Observable Behaviours, and this one little notion can be a wonderful guide in establishing a creative environment where dynamic learning occurs. Here are a few starter tips.

1 It is said that over 80 per cent of any face-to-face communication is non-verbal, so be aware of the non-verbals! Notice students' body language, facial expressions and eye behaviour (position, eye-contact, etc.) as they engage in tasks. Is there any incongruity between what their words say and what their bodies say? Read the signs to ensure that students are comfortable with what you ask them to do.

2 Notice language behaviour. The world of each student will be framed in the metaphors he or she uses. Help to change limiting metaphors that contain limiting beliefs.

3 Notice the students' questioning behaviour. Are you or they asking most of the questions? Are the students' questions divergent, exploratory and self-initiated? Or are they closed and functional so that students can grab hold of your right answers?

4 Use the students' language to make their thinking explicit. What students say is the outcome of what has just gone through their heads. Become increasingly aware of how language reveals underlying thought-processes. (Many of the activities in the rest of this book will add detail to this idea.)

5 Anchor positive behaviours so that students can use them more deliberately (see Idea 31).

Activity: Raise students' awareness of any of the above. For instance, people often ask me about 'writer's block'. I tell them I don't think of it as a block, but as a high hill that allows me to see farther. Encourage students to notice their own and each other's language and adapt unhelpful metaphors.

MAKING LEARNING DYNAMIC

For me the word 'dynamic' means a motivating force. A dynamic teacher is someone who moves his or her students, someone who has an emotional impact so the students 're-member' the lesson positively. But what if, you might well ask, despite all my best efforts the students aren't moved? What if they just can't be bothered to learn? It's a pertinent point, because they'll bring into the classroom just what they will bring, and you can do only what you're able to do. I meet the situation myself all the time, and I'm sustained by the following ideas.

- ○ Enthusiasm communicates. If you love what you're doing the students will know.
- ○ Expectations determine outcomes. Expect the students to do well and they'll endeavour to do their best.
- ○ Students love to think and be creative, especially when they're given clear tasks in a safe environment where individuals' ideas are valued.
- ○ Such tasks promote 'self-initiated behaviour', which enhances learning.
- ○ Successful learning occurs in proportion to how fully students are required to engage their senses.
- ○ New learning occurs as a result of doing something that builds on what has already been learned.
- ○ Learning occurs on many levels – what, where and when, how, why, who (see also Idea 84). 'Why' and 'who' offer the deepest motivational levels for learning: purpose and identity. Our feelings and actions in life are defined by the meanings we make.

Activity: Create opportunities for students to speak about something that enthuses them, ideally linked in a useful way to your subject. Notice how you infuse your teaching with your own enthusiasm for your subject: you're adding impact to the content. Encourage students to take a sincere interest in each others' ideas.

Our motivations, thoughts and actions rise from many levels. When we have an awareness of this we can begin to explore how and why we express ourselves as we do. We can also use our resultant understanding in building strategies to overcome limitations, initiate change and maximize our potential.

A 'neurological levels' model' was developed by Robert Dilts, who is a key figure in the field of neurolinguistic programming (NLP). Robert Dilts proposes that problems can arise – and solutions be sought – at the following levels:

○ *Environment* Where (and when) we are. How we react to our surroundings.
○ *Behaviour* What we do as we fulfil our potential or struggle within our perceived limitations.
○ *Capability* How well we do things (most importantly by our own estimation) and the strategies we use to function in life.
○ *Belief* What we think is true (consciously and/or subconsciously). Beliefs are made of in-formation and can, of course, be limiting or liberating.
○ *Identity* Who we think we are. Our sense of self, core values and 'mission' in life.
○ *Spirit* Why we feel we are here; our sense of relationship to the cosmos and identity-in-purpose.

The first step towards positive change is to identify the level at which the problem occurs. Sometimes both teachers and students put errors, failure in under-standing or bad behaviour down to lack of capability or a 'poor' sense of self-identity. The issue might lie at a more superficial level or, if it does run deep, what has the student 'put together' in his or her life to create such limiting behaviour?

Activity: Notice how students talk about any blocks or limitations to their learning. At what neurological level are they having difficulty? One way of helping them is to identify positivity and resources at the next deepest level. You can also help students to 'reframe' the problem by using metaphor. Help them to think of the difficulty as a creative challenge.

NEUROLOGICAL LEVELS AND CREATIVITY

The idea of 'layeredness' appears often in the field of creativity. The neurological levels' model is one example of it; conscious and subconscious thinking is another, simpler, example. In a very important sense creative thinking is about tapping into the vast resources of memory and imagination, while appreciating that whatever emerges is like the tip of a potential iceberg.

If, for instance, I have an idea for a story, I consciously know at that moment only a tiny fraction of what the whole story will be about. If I think of a new workshop technique, I feel excited to think that beneath that insight can lie many so far hidden variations of the basic idea, which in turn will lead to many other ideas for further workshops! Creative ideas multiply. There are always more where they came from.

The notion of surface structure and deep structure has endless applications. Some are explained in this book – you'll discover many more for yourself. Here's one to play with now . . .

Activity: Have students cut out a triangle of paper about the size of your hand. Draw a line to mark out the top quarter of the triangle. Go to a story – it needn't be one you know – turn to any page and pick a line or two at random. Copy them into the peak of the triangle. Use the rest of the space to jot down whatever comes to mind based on the lines of text – questions, deductions, speculations, etc.

It has often been said, quite correctly, that teachers are not counsellors or therapists. If a student has problems at the level of identity or spirituality, then how can I help him or her, given I have limited time, a syllabus to deliver and around 30 other learners in the class? One of the wisest answers I ever heard came from a chemistry teacher who was renowned as a 'grumpy old man' in the staffroom. He said, 'I allow the children to know that I am a caring presence for them. Even if I get cross with that class, I am a caring presence.' For me this is the platform on which all other strategies for excellence are based.

Whatever happens in students' lives – and we know that some pretty awful stuff can happen – we as teachers can work towards building a safe and caring environment where students' ideas, and students themselves, are valued. For me, guiding principles are:

○ *Keeping the stress low* So many children and adults are frightened of feeling foolish, of getting the answer wrong. A creative attitude says that exploring towards an answer is more educationally valuable than the answer itself. The learning is in the journey.
○ *Increasing the challenge* Learning is more fun if we explore at the limits of our current abilities. A creative and positive tension exists at the edge. If we are too comfortable we grow complacent and bored. If we are pushed beyond current limits too soon we feel threatened and incapable, and we flounder.

Activity: Use this simple anchoring technique to switch on the feel-good factor. Rub the thumb and forefinger of your left hand together (if you're right-handed) whenever you've done something well – and know you have – and feel good about it. Do this every time you are pleased with your achievement. This anchor can then be deliberately used if you find yourself stressed or facing a problem.

1 *Quick feedback* 'Feedback' is a term from the field of cybernetics, where incoming information helps the system to maintain itself most effectively. In an educational context, as teachers we can set precise tasks (though not prescriptive in the limiting sense) that can be accomplished through taking particular steps involving specific kinds of thinking. When students achieve this, telling them quickly that they've done it powers them on to the next challenge. If a student has not achieved the expected outcome, quick feedback again allows for change in the right direction. I am not advocating correction as the main strategy here. There's a huge difference between saying 'Look, that's wrong' and 'Notice what's happened here. I wonder how it can be improved?' (see also Idea 21).

2 *Sincere praise* One meaning of praise is 'to extol the attributes' of something. The overly corrective approach focuses on a lack of attributes or negative ones. Giving sincere praise is a recognition of the positive, while for me the sincerity itself goes to the human heart of what education means. As the old saying goes, 'Catch them doing something right *and tell them so.*'

3 *The principle of utilization* This principle asks you to take whatever the students bring into the classroom and to utilize it positively. Often that's hard work, and sometimes it's impossible, but usually it pays off big time.

Activity: These cool tools can be used by the students themselves. When you have established these strategies in your practice and know that the students benefit from them, point them out to the class and encourage their wider use.

Embedding the creative attitude can be done more effectively when we consider . . .

○ *The principle of potential* Draw a black dot on the whiteboard and ask students what it could be; what it reminds them of. Suggest that when you did this with another group they had twenty ideas about it. When your group has at least that many the students begin to realize that creativity is about seeing the potential in whatever we experience.

○ *The principle of positivity* This is the principle of utilization already mentioned (in Idea 32). Everything has positive value if we're prepared to regard it that way.

○ *The principle of purposefulness* Purpose is experience deliberately and positively applied. In the field of creativity, every idea and insight can lead us in the direction we want to go. All outcomes of our thinking have learning value. Search for examples of how 'dead ends' were actually steps on the road to success – such as Thomas Edison's thousand or so attempts to develop a reliable lightbulb filament.

○ *The principle of 'probable outcomes'* This is also known as the principle of the controlled accident, which means that with some creative thinking of our own we can engineer the learning environment in such a way that our students will have for themselves the insights and discoveries we want them to experience. As the wise old saying has it 'My teacher showed me but I found it by myself'. Review a forthcoming lesson. How can the classroom/lesson content be organized so that students inevitably 'stumble upon' insights for themselves?

○ *The principle of patience* While creativity is not about 'waiting for inspiration to strike' – we can arrange to have ideas when we want them – a degree of patience is required as the subconscious part of the mind processes material into insights. Also, ideas when they appear might not be in their finished form. Take time to mull them over.

Activity: Apply the five P principles from the outset to establish the ethos of creativity.

DEVELOPING EMOTIONAL RESOURCEFULNESS

Creative thinking and emotional resourcefulness are linked. In each case there is a strong relationship between awareness, understanding and control. As we grow more conscious of our feelings (and thoughts that might trigger them) we understand our emotional responses more deeply. Realizing why feelings happen offers opportunities for us to modify them – to change or 'turn down' unpleasant and unhelpful emotions and to boost and strengthen pleasant ones.

The work of Daniel Goleman explores 'emotional literacy' far more deeply. Goleman has taught at Harvard and has written in the fields of behaviour and brain science for the *New York Times*. As a starter, here are a few ideas for developing emotional resourcefulness in yourself and your students.

○ Become more aware of feelings as they occur. Noticing a feeling is the first step towards an intervention.
○ Use the alpha state (see Idea 7) to 'notice quietly' how thoughts link to feelings you experience. Realize that you have more choice about how you can respond. Make clear and deliberate decisions about how you'll react in a given situation.
○ Distinguish between related feelings. How would we express the differences and similarities between, say, envy and jealousy?
○ Anchor positive feelings. A useful little anchor (as we've seen in Idea 31) is to rub your thumb and forefinger together (of your left hand if you're right-handed) each time a pleasant feeling is experienced.
○ Develop classroom anchors to manage emotional states. Stand in a certain spot, for instance, when you give praise (spatial anchor) or use 'mood music' as a precursor to attentive listening or volunteering questions and ideas (auditory anchor).
○ Practise relaxation techniques.

Activity: Think back to a situation that caused unpleasant feelings. If those feelings were music, what would it sound like? Now change the tune in your head and notice how that modifies the feelings.

Strictly speaking, self-esteem is how we estimate ourselves. It is sometimes a cruel irony, however, that both children and adults base their sense of self-esteem on what other people say about them.

That said, students' self-esteem will grow in the right environment, and as teachers we can exert a powerful influence in that arena. Classrooms that foster a creative attitude are also places where self-esteem is likely to flourish.

SELF-ESTEEM AND CREATIVITY

- Use sincere praise. By 'sincere' I mean honest, but it's important that the student recognizes the true link between your praise and the achievement that has earned it. In other words, the student needs to realize for him or herself that they've done well. Your praise then verifies it independently.
- Self-esteem is reinforced by ordinary, everyday experiences. Be aware of the link between the challenges you set and the resilience of the students. Too low a challenge that's effortlessly met will develop self-esteem as poorly as a challenge set too high that therefore leads to failure.
- Use encouraging language (see Idea 21). Adopt a creative attitude yourself and all it implies: explore, experiment and enjoy the field of knowledge; think in terms of processes and strategies rather than just goals and right answers.
- Intervene as appropriate to prevent what can be a downward spiral of limiting beliefs and negative self-talk. Use thinking skills explicitly to 'tease out' the structure of unhelpful thoughts and feelings.
- Anchor achievement. Make your whole classroom a domain where high self-esteem is reinforced by remembered (see Idea 24) positive learning experiences.

This is simply stated but requires creativity and diligence to apply. The acronym means Relevant, Interesting, Naughty and a Giggle.★

Relevance goes back to the old 'what's in it for me?' principle one sees mentioned in books on accelerated learning. Students' motivation is boosted when they appreciate the relevance of the tasks we set for them. This means the immediate relevance of why we ask students to engage in a particular task at that moment and the broader relevance of the learning-to-learn fixed goal of education and in terms of the students' own aspirations for their future. What students don't see as relevant in these ways won't motivate them as much.

Interesting Relevance itself generates interest, but to be 'interested' more generally is an attitude to learning that has deep roots in valuing ideas for their own sake. The creative attitude both presupposes and generates interest in thinking challenges.

Naughty Most dictionaries cast this word in a very bad light to mean 'wayward, wicked, disobedient, blameworthy', etc. But think of it more as mischievous, daring, adventurous, impish, subversive, unconventional – and the tone and intention are caught more precisely. If we regard creativity as 'going beyond the given' a degree of naughtiness helps us to 'step over the line', 'go beyond the comfort zone', 'think outside the box'.

A Giggle Plato made the definitive comment when he said that 'Reason must have an adequate emotional base for education to perform its function'. One of the most powerful emotions (read 'motivators') is laughter.

Activity: Review some of the upcoming tasks you want your students to carry out and modify them (if they need it) in accordance with the RINGtone strategy.

★ I am indebted to my friend Roy Leighton for the RINGtone insight.

It should be clear by now that inspiration is not something we wait around for and hope will strike. Creativity is not vicarious, fickle, unreliable and fleeting. It is fostered and made more powerful by adopting the appropriate attitude focused by strategies that exploit our natural resources of memory and imagination.

When children ask what inspires me, I ask *them* if they have thought about what 'inspiration' means. Usually they haven't. I explain that for me inspiration is the opposite of 'expiration'. When something expires it stops, it is lifeless. Inspiration has, at its heart, that wonderful feeling of being alive, and we can feel most fully alive in that moment of illumination when sudden new understanding occurs.

Inspiration is also linked with 'respiration'. We breathe in the experience of life and breathe out ideas, an expression of our understanding of the world and of ourselves. For me this is linked with education. When I think of that word I take it back through the Latin roots, which are 'to draw out' and 'rear up'. As a teacher I endeavour to draw out the creativity of my students through appropriate strategies, value the expression of their ideas and celebrate their inspirations (their 'breathing forth' of understanding). And in doing so my goal is for them to be 'reared up' and able to stand in the world as independent, creative individuals.

Activity: Ask students what they think 'inspiration' means. Look at inspired work from different subject areas: a powerful poem, a piece of artwork or a scientific discovery. Discuss how inspiration shines out of these things. Show students video clips of scientists, historians, writers, artists, etc. talking excitedly about their field of work. Display inspirational quotes in your classroom (see Idea 120 for examples).

INSPIRATION AND EDUCATION

SECTION

3

The Thinking Toolbox

INTRODUCTION

Thinking is a complex, subtle, elegant and powerful activity. These days I cringe as I recall the times I told a student to 'go and think about it' if he or she was stuck, couldn't figure out an answer, wanted to have an idea, make up a story, etc. That's a bit like telling someone to 'go and make a table' when he or she isn't familiar with the tools in their toolbox or the processes that will result in that particular piece of furniture.

Actually, the 'thinking toolbox' is a metaphor that's often used in connection with the various kinds of thinking of which human beings are capable. Traditionally, thinking skills have been divided into critical and creative. Critical skills are more to do with conscious analysis, reflection and evaluation. Creative skills are more to do with making links, recognizing patterns and generating ideas, with much of the processing being done subconsciously. Sometimes the critical/creative distinction is useful, although I tend to regard it (to change the metaphor) as a bit like exploring the ingredients in my kitchen cupboard – the value of doing this is to use them in combination later.

That said, this book deals more with the creative aspects of thinking, while another in this series, *100+ Ideas for Teaching Thinking Skills*, examines the critical side. Critical thinking tools include: analysing for bias and assumption, attributing, classifying, comparing and contrasting, decision-making, determining cause and effect, drawing conclusions, evaluating, prioritizing, sequencing and solving analogies.

Let's look now in more detail at some creative tools. As we do this, consider how you can apply them in specific subject or other areas of your teaching.

Here is a summary of the main creative thinking skills:

○ *Associating* Making links to create relationships and patterns, and to map out the bigger picture.

○ *Brainstorming (or 'ideas cascade')* Using the subconscious as a resource to help generate a 'melting-pot' of ideas for further consideration.

○ *Evaluating* Judging or deciding upon the comparative worth, value or usefulness of something, by means which may be more *or less* conscious, systematic and deliberate.

○ *Generalizing* Broadening out a statement or viewpoint from consideration of a limited number of particular cases. Creating a broader context from details.

○ *Handling ambiguity and paradox* Reflecting on apparent contradictions/conflicts/opposites and applying strategies to remain tolerant in the face of these and, ultimately, resolve them.

○ *Hypothesizing* Stating a possible position, situation or state from an initial consideration of ideas. Creating explanations that link fragments of evidence.

○ *Inferring* Arriving at conclusions based on subjective assessment of information.

○ *Inventing* Originating something as the product of critical or creative thinking.

○ *Personifying* Using the imagination to associate or identify with an object, creature or concept, and investing it with your personal human qualities to achieve further insight and understanding.

○ *Predicting* Using a range of strategies to anticipate possible outcomes.

○ *Problem-solving* Selecting from a range of critical and/or creative strategies to reach a desired state.

○ *Solving and making analogies* Deepening understanding through the creation of comparisons based on related qualities.

○ *Visualizing* Creating multisensory mental scenarios to deepen understanding.

Activity: Select what you consider to be an educationally rich activity within your subject area and examine it for the range of thinking skills it exercises.

It's fascinating to consider how we think about ideas and the metaphors we use to describe them. We talk about good ideas and bad ones, uplifting ones and depressing ones; we talk about big ideas and bright ideas; there are dangerous ones, earth-shattering ones and groundbreaking ones, which might be simple, complex, straightforward or convoluted. Ideas together can make a flight of fancy and be no more than a figment of the imagination. Ideas can be cool or inflammatory; they might make a point or be cutting-edge. We can use them to take a standpoint or have a slant on a topic. They might be old and tired, or be the brainchildren of which we are very proud . . .

Because thinking is itself such an elusive 'invisible' phenomenon, it is inevitable that we conceive of it in terms of metaphor ('conceive' being a common thinking metaphor). Velcro Thinking (Idea 54) explores this further, but for now consider what a 'rainbow idea' could be like. What would be the qualities of a 'Pegasus idea'? How would 'kitten ideas' behave? What might be the outcomes of 'greenhouse ideas'?

Playing with ideas – and the notion of ideas – in this way is not the same as categorizing them, which is certainly not the same as judging them. Such wordplay can help us to categorize, but its main function is metacognitive; helping students to notice and think about their own thinking.

One simple and useful tool in aiding this is the Ideas Matrix, as in Figure 1 opposite. You can label the axes as you like and need not be constrained by the parameters I chose.

Activity: Ask students where in the matrix would they locate the following ideas?

- ○ Put an uncooked egg in its shell in water to test its freshness. If it floats it's gone off.
- ○ $E = MC^2$
- ○ What is time?
- ○ The Vikings discovered America before Christopher Columbus did.
- ○ Where does the sky end?
- ○ The No. 64 bus goes to the centre of town.

In light of these ideas, how else could you label the parameters of the matrix? What further ideas and questions does this generate?

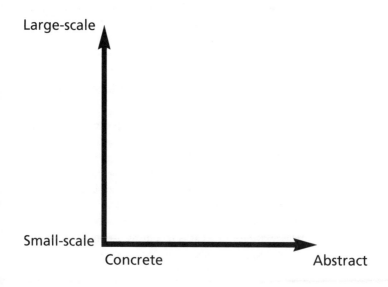

Figure 1: Ideas matrix

ASSOCIATING

To associate is to link or bring together. At a fundamental level our subconscious map of reality is one vast and complex web of associations. The whole purpose and value of being 'in-formed' is that the world should make sense to us. Meaning-making is essentially the creation of links, patterns and networks of ideas.

Some students are described as being 'Big Picture' thinkers or learners, which is to say they like to have an appreciation, an overview, of the whole context of the topic or area of knowledge before making more specific links between details. Other learners, described as 'logical-sequential' thinkers, prefer to link details in order to create the Big Picture as an outcome as they associate specifics to create an overview.

An association of ideas can be 'vast and vague', as when we have a general notion of the geography, history and culture of some distant country, or when we get the 'gist' of a book. Conversely, an association might be 'small and simple', a direct and specific link between concepts, people, objects, etc. Furthermore, associations of either kind can be personal and subjective, general and objective, or somewhere in between.

Immediate applications of our ability to associate could be:

o *Anchoring* (see Ideas 31 and 34) Creating a deliberate link between positive thoughts and feelings and a sound, sight, smell, physical activity, etc. When students associate your classroom (or, more powerfully, yourself) with achievement and success, their learning will flourish.

o *Personalizing knowledge* Encouraging students to boost the relevance of what is taught by asking them to link it with their own lives in terms of goals, reminiscences, anecdotes, etc.

Further strategies for associating appear in Idea 41.

More specifically, the skill of associating can be practised by the following:

○ Creating concept maps. Place a word, for example 'blue', in the centre of a large sheet of paper and have students create a web of links through free association. Subsequently, categorize the responses. How does blue link to flags, for example, or feelings, chemicals, mythology?

○ Concept maps are also a good way of tracking characters in novels, linking them with each other, with settings and events, etc.

○ Allowing students to become familiar with associations expressed in various forms. For example: graphs, bar charts, number patterns in mathematics and cycles in nature depicted visually – the water cycle, the cycle of birth–growth–death, etc.

○ Practising sequencing, generalizing and predicting by having students recognize partial patterns and extrapolating from that point.

○ Looking at advertising and the way in which products are associated with lifestyles, personal qualities and attributes.

○ Studying patterns in language. Notice, for instance, how emotive words (and the associations we make from them) are used for argument and persuasion.

○ Studying associations stated or implied by metaphors in language. For example, how linked words like 'brilliant', 'bright' and 'dull' have traditionally been linked with academic ability.

○ Using students' ability to form associations when examining the concept of symbolism. Study different visual symbols. Create new groups of symbols, where each student links a personal association with the image.

BRAINSTORMING

This is sometimes called 'ideas cascading' and is usually a group activity where many ideas are generated to serve as raw material for later analysis, prioritization and evaluation. Once you have identified the concept(s) to be brainstormed or the problem(s) to be solved, the golden rule is that *all responses are valued and go into the melting-pot.* At this stage no idea is to be evaluated or judged – and certainly not discarded. In this sense brainstorming is a classic example of the situation where there are no right or wrong answers, but only material that will be more or less useful in the end.

Brainstorming is regarded as a creative thinking skill because it relies upon ideas 'popping up' from the subconscious, rather than any conscious figuring-out of solutions. Effective brainstorming requires participants to make links and to look at things in multiple and unusual ways and to volunteer these freely in an uninhibited way. To be in a brainstorming mood is to be in alpha state (see Idea 7), or the dreamer phase of the Disney Strategy (see Idea 18). Planning strategies and realizing solutions, which engage the conscious logical thinking tools, come later.

A well-known example of a brainstorming activity is 'How many uses can you think of for a paper-clip?' (see Idea 43). I remember on one occasion a participant said, 'You could take a million paper-clips and melt them down and use the metal in thousands of ways.' People laughed and the guy felt judged, which was not in the spirit of the exercise. All responses are valued.

This is a great game for establishing the ground-rules of brainstorming. If you're running it with a class, it's a good idea to get someone else to lead the activity while you observe the dynamics of the group, individual students' reactions, etc. The following tips might help to oil the brainstorming machine.

○ Use volunteer scribes to record all ideas.
○ If ideas seem to be drying up, use word-webs and concept-maps to kick-start further associations.
○ Take one response and generalize it to suggest further linked possibilities. So if a student said, 'You could use it as a nose-ring if you were a punk', you might say, 'paper-clips as jewellery. How else could we use it as jewellery?'
○ Encourage humour. Deliberately throw a ridiculous response into the melting-pot. This helps to keep the activity light-hearted and OKs further silly suggestions from the students.
○ Jump into another point of view. Say, for example, 'What ideas would Batman come up with?' Or, 'How would we use paper-clips if we were ants?'
○ Play the 'Criss-Cross' game. What if you crossed a paper-clip with a microchip? What if you crossed a paper-clip with a Swiss army knife? What if you crossed a paper-clip with a thermometer?
○ Combine brainstorming with the 'What if?' game (see Idea 105). What could we use paper-clips for if all colours changed without warning once a week?

HOW MANY USES FOR A PAPER-CLIP?

EVALUATING

This is often regarded as a critical thinking skill because it is through conscious analysis that we identify criteria for judgement, verify and rate answers for accuracy or correctness, review results and solutions in light of their usefulness, etc. However, in a creative environment where ideas are generated within the ethos exemplified by brainstorming, we may choose to 'value it' rather than 'evaluate' in the first instance. I'm also suggesting that evaluating in its broadest sense covers the whole spectrum from objective and precisely defined measurements to the often vague and woolly world of subjective impressions. Consider, for example, how you would evaluate two poems. What criteria can you identify that would allow you to make a judgement about which poem was more powerful, memorable, etc.?

Evaluation, then, can be problematical. So, perhaps a first step in allowing students to become more capable in using this skill is to (a) accept that subjective personal impressions are valuable (indeed, inevitable) in some kinds of evaluation, (b) figure out where along the objective–subjective continuum the evaluation needs to take place and (c) explore the purposes for the evaluation.

Traditionally the steps in an evaluation are:

○ identify criteria involved in the evaluation;
○ prioritize the power and value of the criteria (i.e. evaluate them!);
○ apply the criteria;
○ tally the results;
○ express a judgement, conclusion, etc.;
○ and, finally, review the judgement!

'I never make generalizations' is a well-known and lovely paradox. Practically speaking, all of us do make general statements at some time or other. This is often the result of reactive thinking – knee-jerk opinions that have developed unwittingly over time or which we simply pick up as part of the culture and fail to question. A few of my favourites are 'It never rains but it pours', 'You can't trust people from the South', 'Drivers of sports cars are reckless' (this one often comes down to jealousy!), and the all-time classic, 'Things aren't what they used to be.'

More precisely defined, the ability to generalize is a creative thinking skill; the ability to form a broad statement, viewpoint, rule or summary based on a sampling of instances. This is *reflective generalization*, rather than the reactive examples quoted above. Generalizations of this kind, however, can still fall along the objective–subjective continuum for evaluation. Personal opinions can and do still have value in many cases.

The steps to forming a reflective generalization are:

○ gather the information/examples you want to work with;
○ search for any patterns that already exist;
○ identify any new patterns you uncover;
○ clarify trends suggested by these patterns;
○ test the validity of your predictions (ask around, look at the trend later to see how it's developed, etc.);
○ judge the validity of your generalization.

Try these with your class:

○ predict next year's fashions;
○ discuss the development of a writer's style;
○ invent new proverbs after looking at old ones;
○ guess what films might be popular in two years' time;
○ predict your own achievements in ten years' time.

HANDLING AMBIGUITY AND PARADOX

My next statement will be the truth. My last statement was a lie.

Accelerated-learning theory suggests that students' learning develops more quickly when they feel comfortable with ambiguity, uncertainty and paradox. Many of the activities that we've already looked at (and most we have yet to explore) highlight the fact that a creative attitude works best in a field where answers are not right or wrong (yet) and where all ideas are valued because they are pregnant with unrealized potential. Besides this, life itself is full of uncertainty and ambiguity. Conscious, logical thinking tools are quite often not the best way of dealing with life's twists and turns. At the deepest (spiritual) level, sometimes the viewpoint that life is a journey to be enjoyed rather than a problem to be solved* is the healthiest way of being.

Needing to know the right answer right now seems to be an imperative of the current educational regime, but it can lead to the limiting behaviour of 'grasping and telling'. Students who grasp and tell hang on to the facts teachers give them and take every opportunity to let you know that they know these things. On the surface this can look like showing off, but underneath there is the fear of looking foolish for being wrong, silly or out of the ordinary.

Establishing a creative attitude in students limits this unhealthy behaviour and, *per se*, helps students to feel comfortable with contradictions. More formally, handle ambiguity by:

○ identifying contradictions;
○ listing PIN points – positive, interesting, negative – for each side of the contradiction;
○ arguing positively for each point of contradiction;
○ reaching conclusions that demonstrate your acceptance and appreciation of the contradictory situation and express a win/win outcome.

* Quotation from Alan Watts.

The word 'hypothesis' traces back to the Greek meaning 'a foundation; to place under' – in this sense to lay a foundation of ideas on which possible explanations can be built, tested, verified or falsified. It is a web of supposition, not yet taken to be true or otherwise, that acts as a basis for further reasoning. Hypothesizing is sometimes classed as a creative skill because its aim is to generate possibilities, but practically speaking, as those possibilities arise they tend to be at least partially evaluated against previous experience and 'common sense'. Hypothesizing, to my mind, lies on the borderline of the creative and the critical, and uses thinking tools in combination.

If you're working with younger students a device called the 'Maybe Hand' is a good way to introduce hypothesizing. Begin by observing a phenomenon that needs to be explained, for example, 'I notice that smoke usually rises.' Hold out your hand palm upwards. The observation is located in the centre. Each finger represents a possible explanation. So, smoke usually rises because . . .

○ Maybe sunlight attracts it.
○ Maybe it's lighter than air.
○ Maybe what I've seen is a coincidence and sometimes smoke falls.
○ Maybe it's warm and heat rises.
○ Maybe the wind blows it upwards.

You can now say to the group, 'Look, we have a handful of treasures (hypotheses) to explore further.' The next step of the process will be to evaluate each possibility (see Idea 44).

One way of developing students' ability to hypothesize is to regard possible explanations of observed phenomena as stories. Hypothesizing then becomes a story-making game. Take the following example:

o the kitchen skylight window is open;
o the teacloth that covered the plate on the worktop is on the floor;
o the plate has nothing on it;
o there are grease-marks on the worktop;
o the family cat does not appear when her name is called.

Now pose the question, 'What stories can we make up that use all of these pieces of evidence?' First, notice how easy it is to jump to conclusions. Obviously the family cat jumped in through the skylight window, ate the meat on the plate and has disappeared to sleep it off! Well, that's one possibility, but not the only one.

Use the 'Maybe Hand' (see Idea 47) to explore alternatives. Suggest one or two outrageous or radical possibilities . . . miniature aliens flew in through the skylight, teleported the meat on the plate to Alpha Centauri 4 and vapourized the cat when it tried to attack them. Sometimes the craziest ideas turn out to be truth.

Develop hypothesizing by playing the 'Why?' game. Invite students to ask why-questions that tantalize them, such as the following:

o Why do other primates have more hair than we do?
o Why is Cardiff the capital of Wales?
o Why is the Sahara Desert spreading?
o Why does the Moon have big grey 'seas' on its Earth-facing side but not on the other side?
o Why do cats have whiskers?
o Why did the Romans build such straight roads?
o Why is Shakespeare regarded as one of the world's greatest playwrights?

Create and then test hypotheses that answer these questions.

Some sources make no distinction between an *inference*, an *assumption* and a *deduction*, since all of them involve arriving at a conclusion. However, I do think each works in a rather different way in terms of the thinking that goes on.

For me a *deduction* means reaching a conclusion by noticing clues or amassing evidence from without – being able to work things out logically and objectively based on what's actually there.

An *assumption* is a conclusion that's reached in the absence (wholly or largely) of outside evidence. Mr Smith has arrived home at 5 p.m. for the past few days. I assume he will do the same today. There may be no evidence present to support my conclusion; I'm going entirely upon my memories of what has happened. Assumptions are sometimes accurate, of course, but can lead to a dangerous habit of thought. Educationally and socially it's worth asking students, 'What clues did you notice that led you to say that?' if you think they have made an unwarranted assumption.

Now if, on Mr Smith's fifth day, I notice that at 4.55 p.m. the gates to his driveway and garage doors are open, and that Mrs Smith is standing in the front porch looking impatiently at her watch, and there's a smell of cooking coming from the kitchen, then I can *infer* that Mr Smith will indeed, as usual, be arriving home soon. I can't deduce it, because those 'outside clues' don't point unequivocally to *Mr Smith's* arrival, but by 'reading between the lines' I can expect my *inference* to be accurate.

Activity: Ask students to notice examples of things in their own lives or environment that have led them into making inferences: I see a house with a burglar alarm and infer there are valuable things inside; I notice a person driving a people-carrier and infer the driver has a large family; I see someone dressed in denim and leather and infer he or she likes hard rock music.

Inventing is regarded as a creative thinking skill in so far as it is a deliberate, more or less systematic, generation of ideas as part of a search to solve problems. The thing that's invented is, of course, the outcome that lies at the far end of the Disney Strategy (see Idea 18); but inventing as a process relies heavily upon a creative attitude and use of the subconscious.

The roots of the word 'invent' are 'to come upon, to find', which suggests that we almost stumble upon solutions accidentally. It's true that serendipity – a happy accident – can play a part in the solution, but as I have tried to suggest, creativity is not some mysterious mental alchemy. Inventors (in whatever field) are, to paraphrase the dictum, 'perpetual notion machines', and it is more usually true that discovery favours the prepared mind.

Educationally we can encourage the generation of ideas in our students by applying the *narrative-dynamic model* to our teaching. The structure of a narrative is:

○ Orientation: becoming familiar with the domain of the learning; getting the Big Picture.
○ Complication: finding a problem in that field which stimulates a search towards the solution.
○ Resolution: the re-solution of, or more useful answer to, the problem.

In other words, the emphasis of the narrative-dynamic way of learning is different from the more traditional model of objectives–content–methodology–evaluation. Both strategies of course can form part of the teacher's educational toolkit.

Many of the activities in this book focus on invention. Look especially at the 'Merlin' game (Idea 98) and the 'What if?' game (Idea 105) to set the ball rolling.

To personify can mean to invest a concept, object or animal with human qualities, or by a leap of the imagination to identify with that thing – mentally to *become* the concept, object or animal – and see the world from its point of view.

Personifying is a creative thinking skill because information is drawn off the subconscious map in a focused and deliberate way and is filtered through your understanding of the thing with which you're identifying. This is one example of a general mental mechanism called *perceptual filtering.* Our perceptions of the world tend to be filtered through our values and beliefs (conscious and subconscious) to create a subjective viewpoint that can be limiting or liberating to various degrees. If we fail to realize this and reflect on it, then the way we look at the world can become a mindset – a mind 'set' – a hardening of the categories that traps us into that single perspective.

Personifying immediately helps to create other perspectives, which is an essential aspect of a creative attitude. As a life-skill, personifying trains empathy. Mental flexibility leads to emotional flexibility, so we can imagine how the world looks through someone else's eyes.

Personifying is also a fun way, and often an effective way, of solving problems and reaching new understandings. Because we learn best by doing, when we identify with an object and *are* that object, the learning experience is all the more powerful. I once saw a science lesson where groups of children danced around holding hands. They were starch molecules. Other classmates came and broke the groups apart. They were enzymes. I never forgot that lesson, and I daresay the students haven't either.

Try these activities with your class:

○ Take an emotion such as envy or anticipation. If that emotion were a person, what might she or he look like?
○ Work with students to create role-play scenarios for various natural phenomena, such as the rain-cycle, the Moon orbiting the Earth orbiting the Sun, or the evolution of life from simple to more complex organisms.

PERSONIFYING

○ Personify different substances, such as diamonds, water, fire and wood. Speak as though you were that substance. What are your strengths and weaknesses? What does the world look like to you?

It is deeply ironic, I think, that as human beings we have solved countless problems with the power of our brains but created countless others. The world, I suppose, will never be problem-free. We will always have need of solutions.

Problem-solving is conventionally classed as a creative thinking skill because although solutions are sometimes reached through logical and linear methodologies, more often than not we rely on sudden insights, intuitions, illuminations and hunches to bring about the breakthroughs we need. Potential solutions are often processed subconsciously before conscious solutions occur.

As a general strategy, when a problem needs to be solved:

o Define it clearly. Break it down into smaller parts if possible.
o Identify outcomes. What will a solution look like, feel like, etc.?
o Be goal-oriented. Maintain a positive intention that the problem *will be solved*.
o Think strategically. Use a number of ways of tackling the problem – many of the activities in this book make effective problem-solving strategies.
o Give yourself pre-processing time. In other words, let your subconscious mind work on the problem. Sometimes this means backing off and doing something else. Constant conscious engagement often leads to frustration.
o Notice results, insights, inklings and feelings. Make a point of noting down what you remember of dreams. The answer may be disguised there.
o Notice your perceptions. The desire to solve a problem often 'filters' the world very specifically: 'selective noticing' can bring ideas to mind so startlingly that it feels uncanny.
o Be cool. As the old Arabian proverb tells us, 'The situation is impossible, but not serious.'

PROBLEM-SOLVING

Apply the strategy outlined in Idea 46, and use any of the tools in this book to arrive at creative solutions to the problems listed below.

○ A supermarket chain wants to boost its sales by 10 per cent this year to get ahead of the competition.

○ A gifted and talented student in your school is deliberately underachieving so as not to 'stand out in the crowd'. He or she just wants to lead a normal life.

○ The local police force wishes to reduce opportunist burglaries in your area.

○ Another pupil wants to study more effectively to get the best grades possible in the forthcoming exams.

○ Lack of parking space has become a problem in the town of Kenniston.

○ The school librarian (Learning Resources Coordinator?) wants to replace the Dewey Decimal System for cataloguing books with something better.

○ My four cats keep scratching at our furniture, wallpaper and doors. They're ruining the house, but I can't bear to get rid of them. Help me!

Activity: Ask the students to think of other problems to practise the solve-it strategy. Select different scales of problem to work with; it could be something to do with the school or neighbourhood, or a global issue that concerns everyone.

In Idea 39 (Ideas matrix) we touched upon the way we think about ideas themselves. The vocabulary and metaphors that we conventionally use can be useful but may also be limiting. Playing with the metaphors for ideas will usually provide new insights about them, and frequently suggest new and more effective thinking strategies.

On one occasion when I was speaking to a class about creative writing, the teacher asked, 'But what do you do when you get a writing block, when you hit that barrier?' I said, 'I put a door in it and walk through!' Then I asked the students how they might overcome such a barrier and these 10-year-olds told me we could use a trampoline, a rocket-pack, a hot-air balloon, ride on Pegasus or grow wings ourselves and fly over. This point is important when we reflect on what message that teacher was communicating by talking about 'blocks' and 'barriers' to thinking. Creating liberating metaphors, such as these students were eager and able to do, can not only suggest strategies for, *but also presuppose many alternative strategies and solutions*.

With that in mind, we can build on our 'solve-it toolkit' by increasing our repertoire of thinking metaphors. We already talk about 'flexible thinking' or 'blinkered thinking'. These indicate strategies or ways of thinking. But the supply of comparisons is endless . . .

Activity: How would ideas work together in Velcro thinking? What would be the advantages of binocular thinking? How could pizza thinking help? Where would bob-sled thinking be most effective? What other thinking metaphors come to mind now?

VELCRO THINKING

SOLVING AND MAKING ANALOGIES

An analogy is a comparison based on shared qualities, (usually) of two things running in parallel. The point of creating analogies is often to clarify concepts by making them more concrete and 'visualizable'. A simple pattern for constructing analogies is:

A is like *B* because both of them . . .

So:

o Time is like a river because both flow in one direction.
o A life is like a story because both have a beginning, middle, end, chapters, characters, events, etc.
o The mind is like a butterfly because both touch lightly on many things.

Another pattern for analogies is:

A is to *B* as *C* is to *D*.

So:

o Water is to liquid as rock is to solid.
o Descend is to depth as ascend is to height.
o Hearing is to ear as sight is to eye.

Relationships, and therefore analogies, come in many kinds. Here are some common ones:

o Object/composition: shoe is to leather as coat is to . . .
o Part/whole: branch is to tree as stream is to . . .
o Object/function: knife is to cut as shovel is to . . .
o Moderate/extreme: sadness is to grief as fright is to . . .
o Opposites: hot is to cold as high is to . . .
o Specific/general: cat is to mammal as lizard is to . . .

Activity: Ask your class to create an analogy by picking the two things you wish to compare (usually an abstract concept and a concrete object), to identify the similarities and to construct the comparison by following your chosen pattern.

Visualizing refers to the ability we have to imagine with images. Accelerated learning theory talks about visual, auditory or kinaesthetic orientations in learners, but most often the emphasis on one above the other is, I think, a habit of thought rather than any basic lack of capability. Furthermore, because vision is our only truly long-distance sense, with around 90 per cent of the information we receive coming in through our eyes, the subconscious map of reality is largely visual. It is for this reason also that *visual organizers* for information allow students to retain and remember information more readily than pages of text.

So, although we can all visualize, it is a skill that can be refined and developed with practice. Many of the activities explored in this book make use of visualizations more or less explicitly. Begin by using these especially useful exercises with your class:

○ *Changing point of view* Imagine how the world looks from a different viewpoint – sitting on the roof of a house, looking out from a manhole, standing on your head, etc.

○ *Overview* Use concrete examples like looking down on your town from 3,000 feet, and abstract examples like the rise and fall of the Roman Empire (what components will you put together to visualize that?).

○ *Multisensory visualization* When you look at a picture, what sounds do you imagine are in there? What smells? What textures?

○ *Time-hops* Look at a picture and jump forward and backward in time. What changes?

○ *Fast forward/rewind* Turn time-hops into a movie. Speed up time forwards, then backwards. What do you notice? Now run the movie backwards and forwards in slow motion.

○ *Thought experiment* Get radical, as Einstein did. Imagine what the universe would look like if you rode on a lightbeam, or were a molecule, a blood cell, etc.

INSIGHT PROBLEMS

Some problems can be solved by applying conscious logical thinking skills, while solutions to others suggest themselves in an Aha! moment of illumination. The mind works quickly and much of the mental processing we do happens at a subconscious level. Put those two ideas together and you have what has been called the Eureka Effect, which generates 'insight solutions'. In other words, sometimes rather than trying to solve problems logically, we can simply notice solutions that spring fully formed to mind.

My experience has been that insight thinking works a bit like the 'magic eye' pictures that were very popular some years ago. By staring through the pictures, as it were, they suddenly leapt into 3D clarity. Sometimes I found it worked easily for me, sometimes after a while and sometimes not at all. Insight thinking feels a bit the same.

Activity: Consider, for instance, the following puzzles:

1 You are invited to purchase an antique coin dated 540 BC for a very reasonable price. Should you buy it?
2 Four people are playing a game around a table. But they all lose. No other people are present. How can this be?
3 Describe how you can put 27 animals into four pens so that there is an odd number of animals in each pen.

In my case the answer to 1 sprang to mind at once; 2 took a while to occur to me, while I didn't get the solution to 3 at all. And in case you were wondering . . .

Answers
1 BC wasn't used before Christ, so the coin is a fake.
2 All four people are playing solitaire.
3 Put three smaller pens inside a fourth larger pen and you can then have an odd number of animals inside each smaller pen.

Type 'insight puzzles' into a search engine for lots more examples.

Games and Activities: Visual Literacy

THE METAPHOR GAME

Metaphor is deeply embedded in our language ('deeply embedded' being one example) and is a powerful determinant of our attitudes and beliefs, and therefore perceptions. The metaphors we use to frame our understanding largely define that understanding. If the metaphors are not chosen, or remain unchallenged, then we live in a cage of our own making.

A couple of examples stand out in my memory. An acquaintance of mine was going through a period of depression and said to me: 'Do you know Steve, that when you're depressed like I am, the future is a long dark tunnel with no light at the end.' What struck me more than the tunnel image was the fact that this person envisaged the future *in the singular*, leaving no option but to travel that long dark tunnel. On another occasion a friend was trying to quit smoking. She said: 'You know, it's like pushing a huge boulder uphill. As soon as you relax, that boulder rolls right back down to where it started!'

I said back to her, 'Why don't you tilt the whole landscape the other way so the boulder rolls to the top by itself?' She laughed, but gave it a go – and a week later announced that she was a non-smoker.

Try these ideas with your class:

o If the day you're having were a household object, what would it be?
o When you talk about the future, what do you compare it with?
o Think of a difficulty you have at school. What kind of animal would it be?
o Now think of the animal that you would choose to compare with the solution?

Am I suggesting that by controlling our metaphors we can have greater control in our lives? Absolutely.

Activity: Help to develop the creative attitude in your students by playing the metaphor game. Pick a topic or theme and begin. 'The mind is a butterfly because . . . It's a web because . . . It's a rocketship because . . . It's a tree because . . . It's a river because . . . It's the moon because . . .'

The picture over the page, *The Walker* (Figure 2), was drawn by my friend, the artist Chris Pepper. Ask students to take a look and jot down their first impressions. Now encourage them to notice the thinking they did to make those notes. What struck them first? What questions came to mind as they studied the picture? Did they find themselves making up stories about the striding figure?

Metacognition, you'll recall, means thinking about the thinking you do. Members of my local writers' group made comments like:

○ He's being followed. I think he stole that bag. It's got jewellery inside.
○ He looks very shifty. I don't trust him.
○ The scene is set long ago, in the Middle Ages or something.
○ There's a strange tower in the background, and the clouds around the moon look weird.
○ He's looking at someone down that alley – a hooded figure, tall and thin, with a menacing air about him.
○ There's an inn nearby – I noticed the bottle and barrel. I can hear lots of noise coming from inside the pub.
○ I think the man's a werewolf. The full moon has come from behind the clouds and he's just about to change!
○ It's a well-drawn picture, but I don't like this fantasy stuff myself.

Now let's look at metaphor, and then again at the tools we have in the thinking toolbox, and why a picture like this provides such a rich field for developing creativity.

Figure 2: *The Walker* © Chris Pepper

The picture activity in Idea 59 can be used across all ages and abilities. I have found that students who might struggle academically often shine in these circumstances, where 'right answers' are not the only measure of success, where clear thinking tasks are required and where creative challenge is increased within an environment of low risk or threat.

Having begun the students' exploration of the picture, continue by saying, 'I want you to be nosy. Look at this picture and notice something about it, anything at all. And when you've done that, tell me what it is you've noticed.'

You are already building your creative environment. Notice what you've said:

o You've encouraged and reinforced the value of 'nosiness'.
o You've asked for a precise thinking task – simple observation/notice and tell.
o You've used the neutral word 'notice' rather than 'see', which is sense-specific.
o You've started with a low-challenge task. It's easy to notice *something*, so less confident students are tempted to join in.
o You've used the word 'when', which is a presupposition of success. Most of the students won't consciously have been aware of that 'when' and won't reflect on it (which might have led some of them to doubt it). But all will subconsciously react to your expectation that success is inevitable.

Your students are likely to give you the same kind of responses as the people in my writers' group (see Idea 59), the comments expressing a range of different thoughts. An important function of this activity is to separate out *what else* is going on in the students' minds as well as simple observation.

THE THINKING COMES OUT IN THE LANGUAGE

Any spoken response is the outcome of the thinking that preceded it. When your students examine the picture on p. 68, what they say will be full of clues as to what's just gone on in their heads. We'll be examining this range of thinking tools shortly, but for now we'll concentrate on:

○ *Association* Some students are likely to be reminded of other things as they look at the picture. To 're-mind' is 'to bring again into cognitive space'. Memories have been evoked, although sometimes we don't know at that moment what it is that's sparked the recollection.

○ *Tentativeness* Some students will have clear impressions and ideas but express them cautiously, often using words like would, should, might, possibly, probably, etc. Frequently this is not speculation: the student is hedging his or her bets. 'I should think that the man might be in a hurry.' There is a subtext here, which goes something like, 'I'm telling you I *should* think it, but I'm not necessarily thinking it because I could be wrong. So don't be annoyed with me if I'm wrong because I've already told you I might be wrong!'

In these situations I say, 'Take "should" and "might be" and throw them away. What have you just thought about the man?' When the student says, 'He's in a hurry', then I say, 'Well done. You've confidently told me about the thoughts you've clearly had in your head.'

And that's an important learning which needs to be reinforced. In a creative classroom, the ideas we have must be valued.

A common response to picture exploration is the student who 'spins a yarn', making up a story there and then to explain what he or she sees in the picture. 'Well I think this man has just mugged someone in the alley and stolen his money. The mugger needs money because he's travelling across this country in search of the man who stole away the woman he loved.'

This student's imagination is running away with him or her, as the saying goes. At this point I explain that we can all spin yarns. We do it as easily as a spider spins a thread. And it's easy to let your imagination run away with you. But pretend your imagination is a horse and you are the rider. That horse is more powerful than you are, but you have the reins. So you can run away with your imagination, but you wouldn't let that horse gallop around anywhere it wants to.

An effective way of reining-in 'the vigorous horse of the mind' is to focus the students' attention on clues, on specific evidence for the statements that we make. There are no clues that the walker in the picture has mugged anyone (let alone that the victim is male). We can infer that he's in a hurry because of the length of his stride, and also that what's in the bag is small, but we can't deduce it because the bag might be empty. But to say that it's money is a speculation. In fact we can deduce very little from the picture, but we can infer plenty – and speculate endlessly.

Activity: As the students make statements about the picture, invite them to go back and look for the clues which led them to that conclusion.

The word 'speculate' goes back to the Latin roots meaning 'to spy out' and 'watchtower'. For me this creates an image of gazing down from a height, looking in all directions to gain an overview detached, as it were, from the possibilities that you see. I think that's a useful description of the mental structure of speculation.

We have seen elsewhere (see Idea 47) how the 'Maybe Hand' gives students an easy and concrete way of considering several possibilities. With reference to our picture resource, we notice the man walking quickly along the deserted street. From that initial observation we can speculate that

○ he's running away from pursuers;
○ he's lost and searching nervously for a familiar street;
○ he's cold, so walking quickly;
○ he's stolen whatever is in the little bag;
○ he's about to commit some criminal act.

After collecting a 'handful of treasures' we can tease out clues to support these different possibilities, combining them with the logical-linking word 'because' (see Idea 85). So, maybe he's stolen whatever's in the little bag because he looks shifty and guilty. But also look for clues that support other possibilities. Maybe he hasn't stolen it because I notice that he's holding the bag out in the open.

Note that the 'Maybe Hand' can also be used in other subject areas, for example to list key variables in scientific experiments.

Activity: Observing what happens to sugar crystals in water. As the teacher you could say, 'We're going to notice what happens when we place sugar crystals in water. Using the Maybe Hand, what do you think might affect what happens to the crystals?'

The students might respond:

○ Maybe the temperature of the water.
○ Maybe the size of crystal.
○ Maybe some movement in the water.
○ Maybe the length of time the crystals are in the water.
○ Maybe other things placed in the water with the crystals.

A famous writer was once asked what were the three most important pieces of advice for developing a good imagination. The reply was 'Visualize. Visualize. Visualize!' Our mental map of reality is largely visual. Despite many people's conscious habit of being predominantly visual, auditory or kinaesthetic (or a combination) we can all draw upon remembered imagery and bring pictures into our 'mind's eye'. Visualization is an important skill that, like most mental skills, can be developed further. Consider the following lapses of visualization:

○ Running into the room, he threw open the window as he switched on the light.
○ Williams saw the chaos in the street below and rubbed his nose, wondering what it would sound like.

And my all-time favourite:

○ Her eyes twinkled, fluttered, met his, dropped to the floor then went back to the jewels. He picked them up, held them for a moment then returned them to her with a smile.

Activity: These 'insight problems' (see Idea 57) can also be solved by visualizing the scene in various ways:

1 John is facing east and Paul is facing west. John says to Paul, 'You look a little pale today.' How is this possible?
2 Using ten matches, arrange them into two squares of different sizes using all of the matches. (You are not allowed to break any.)
3 A little boy went to the zoo. When he went to school the next day his teacher asked him what he saw. The boy said, 'I only saw ostriches and giraffes. There were 30 eyes and 44 legs.' One of his classmates shouted out, 'I know exactly how many ostriches and giraffes he saw!' How did the classmate work it out?

VISUALIZATION CHALLENGES

Answers

1 John and Paul are facing one another.

2 Make a square using eight matches. Fit the other two inside the square in a corner.

3 Visualize the fronts of the ostriches and giraffes. Thirty eyes equals fifteen fronts – using up 30 front legs, leaving fourteen hind legs. They will belong to seven giraffes. The other eight fronts must belong to ostriches.

An 'obserpinion' is an observation that's 'welded' to a reflex opinion which remains unchallenged. We came across something similar when we looked at generalizations (see Idea 45). If we fail to reflect on the value-judgements we make, they lead to a 'hardening of the categories', which then over time 'bleed out' across the map of reality. Referring again to *The Walker* (Figure 2, p. 68), notice the way the process might develop.

1 *Observation* I notice a man apparently walking quickly along a deserted street. He's pulling his tunic more closely about himself. He's carrying a small bag.
2 *Obserpinion* He's a shifty-looking one. He's up to no good, if you ask me.
3 *Generalization* You can't trust people if you can't see their eyes.

Generalized obserpinions represent a highly filtered and often limited way of looking at the world. We can counter this tendency in various ways.

○ Being metacognitive. Catching ourselves in the act of thinking such thoughts.
○ As the philosopher Alfred North Whitehead said, 'We think in generalities, but we live in detail.' Notice the particular details of experience. Use *vivid particularities* (see Idea 111) to impress the uniqueness and diversity of events upon the mind.
○ Use 'because' to stick reasons on to what we say and think. 'You can't trust people if you can't see their eyes because . . .' at the very least gives us pause for reflection. Failure to come up with reasons might cause us to abandon an unhelpful opinion.
○ Use precise questioning. What *exactly* leads me/you to think that?

Activity: Scan newspaper and magazine articles for generalizations and obserpinions. Look for evidence in the article to support such statements. A more challenging version of this activity is to look for obserpinions in textbooks. Also, select a science topic and compare the way it's written up in a modern textbook and one from several decades ago.

'OBSERPINIONS'

RESPONSIBILITY AND CREATIVITY

A creative attitude leads us to see the world in different ways. Creativity means getting into the habit of adopting multiple perspectives, coming in at odd angles, thinking outside the box – and indeed dipping into various boxes to make new combinations. Because thoughts and feelings are linked, how we think affects how we feel. Generalized obserpinions will always evoke the same feeling response . . .

So, I'm travelling along the motorway. Suddenly a sleek silver saloon cuts me up dangerously and, without indicating, zooms away up the slip road. Automatically I think, 'Stupid BMW drivers. They're all mad!' and I'm filled with road-rage and indulge in violent wishful daydreams about what I'd like to do to that guy!

Or . . . The same event occurs. The silver BMW cuts me up and hurtles away. But if I now have the presence of mind to catch myself in the act of thinking I can create a mental Maybe Hand. Maybe that particular driver, who happens to be in a BMW, is an idiot on the road. Maybe he's a businessman who's rushing to a vital meeting. Maybe his wife is lying critically ill in hospital and he's racing to be by her side . . .

If I have the wit to reflect on these options I can choose one to accept or believe in (feeling comfortable with the uncertainty of never knowing the right answer). And if I choose my thinking response I have more control of my emotional response. I do not need to be a victim of my automatic feelings. This takes us to the heart of responsibility, which is the ability we have to respond.

Activity: Try these with your students:

○ You notice a young man in scruffy clothes and with untidy hair running down the street clutching a woman's handbag.
○ You notice two people across the street. They laugh. One of them looks at you. The two laugh again.
○ You notice someone who is clearly overweight walking into a cakeshop.

When the hypnotherapist David Lesser delivered a lecture he would always do so with a large sign on the wall behind him which said, 'I am responsible for what I say, but not for what you hear.' Good advice that also applies more generally to the ways in which we can distort how we experience the world. Help your students to understand some common so-called *cognitive distortions*.

○ *All-or-nothing thinking*, where the world is good or bad, where things are black or white, where if something isn't a total success then it's a complete failure.

○ *Labelling* Putting a label on yourself or others 'freezes' them in your mind, creating a 'hardening of the categories'. 'I'm useless' puts you in a state; makes you static, as it were, a frozen category. Labelling combined with generalization exacerbates the problem. 'The rich are right-wing', for example.

○ *Negative filtering* This kind of selective perception plucks out certain aspects of experience and gives them a negative spin. The glass is not only half empty, but it gets knocked over and smashes!

○ *Mind-reading* Making assumptions about someone else's thoughts that lead you to jump to negative conclusions. 'She's quiet today. I bet she's still angry about what I said yesterday. She'll probably finish with me now . . .'

○ *Should–but barriers* 'Should' and 'but' often go together, even if the 'but' isn't stated. Should–but thinking blocks possibilities and further progress.

A creative attitude, through the active and deliberate use of the imagination, helps to counter such cognitive distortions very effectively.

Activity: Invite students to note down cognitive distortions that they catch themselves using, or which they hear from other people.

COGNITIVE DISTORTIONS

Let's return to our picture on p. 68. Another educational function of picture exploration is to practise using the imagination in a multisensory way, as obviously we absorb information about the world through all of our senses. When we represent ('re-present') our experience in cognitive space, most people favour one sensory mode above the others. This, I feel, is just a habit rather than some deepseated neurological process.

Using the picture, if you invite students to 'see the picture in colour. Turn up the colours in your head and tell me when you've noticed them', some students will respond immediately. As their hands go up (or however their responses are indicated), their behaviour is telling you that they can clearly and easily do visual processing. These students are likely to be the more visually-oriented learners, the ones who like visual support as they learn.

Ask them about the colours they imagine. Be aware of the following:

o The use of hand movements and other body language as they speak. When this happens I say, 'Look at that, you're doing something really intelligent, using your hands to help you to visualize those colours more clearly.'

o The way students' eyes move to access imagined visual information. Neurolinguistic Programming (NLP) theory indicates that visual thinkers tend to move their eyes upward.

o Tentative, cautious responses and 'should–but' limiters (see Idea 67).

o Details of language. If a student says, for example, 'the sky has a reddish tint', ask the group what effect that 'ish' has on the way they imagine the colour.

In studying black-and-white visual images, some students will not respond to your encouragement to see colours because their 'default response' might be in some other sensory mode. Even as certain students talk readily about colours, others are more clearly hearing sounds in the picture. So at some point in the activity ask the whole group to 'turn up the sounds coming out of the picture, and when you've heard them tell me what they are'. (Notice the 'when', which is a presupposition of success.)

Auditorily-oriented thinkers now come to the fore, together with those visual thinkers who can do sounds with equal facility. Of course, as more students take part in this activity *all of them* are being exposed to multi-sensory mental processing, which is one of your aims.

While students tell you about their impressions of sound from the picture, steadily raise the creative challenge by enquiring about the different 'submodalities' or smaller details of the sound. How long is the sound? Is it continuous or broken? What about the volume? How high is it pitched? Is it a pure sound, many combined sounds or discordant? What can you compare it to (use of simile and metaphor)? Is it metallic, glassy, etc.? What feelings does the sound draw out in you?

Move on to build up a 'sonic landscape' within the picture, which adds an important new dimension to what the students are seeing. As you develop their auditory acuity in this way, transfer the skill to other areas.

JUMP IN

Another aspect of studying visual images is to raise awareness of physical, or kinaesthetic, impressions. Build on what the students have already offered from the last few Ideas by saying, 'Now I'm going to count to three. On the count of three I want you to jump into that picture, stand in that street and then you can notice something new. Here we go . . . one, two, three!'

In framing the task in this way you've used two powerful techniques to stimulate the imagination.

1 Notice the pause between explaining the task and then beginning it. In those few moments the students will be *pre-processing* possible responses; that is, subconsciously gathering up from their map of memory impressions that may be useful when they jump into the picture.

2 Notice also how you described the whole mental task very precisely – so the students knew exactly what to do, but you left the outcomes vague. You didn't give any indication really of what kinds of things they will notice. This technique is called *artful vagueness*. The precision of the task you've set is a useful support to the students' thinking but allows enough creative space for them to have their own ideas. This demonstrates flexibility within a structure.

Now some other students may join in, and their impressions are likely to be more tactile and referenced to the body. They will tend to talk about temperature, texture, weight, movement and direction. Also, their hand movements may be more exaggerated. These students are more likely to want to learn by doing in a more overtly physical way.

Lack of concentration is a big problem in many schools. It's also a problem with many causes, I'm sure. However, most people have the potential to concentrate for long periods and can train themselves to do so. Obviously we all need periods of 'downtime', when our mental state shifts and we disengage a little and 'go into ourselves' to process what's been happening, in readiness to go back into the world in 'uptime' with our concentration refreshed.

One way of developing longer periods of concentration in students is to give them tasks with some variety and diversity built in. Picture exploration accommodates this: the students are being asked to do many different kinds of thinking, and rather than being allowed just to fall back on their routine skills, they are being constantly stimulated and challenged.

You may well find that a group can be kept engaged for 30, 40, 50 minutes or longer in this activity. However, if time is at a premium you can break it down into smaller units. On one occasion do ten minutes of notice and tell, picking out the kinds of thinking the students do. Some time later, look at colours; later still, sounds. Maybe weeks later, jump into the picture for further impressions. The students are likely to (re-)member what they've done before in a positive way, because their ideas have been valued. Also, because you're developing their creative thinking abilities, which can then be applied across the curriculum, the activity has great educational value.

ENGAGEMENT THROUGH VARIETY AND DIVERSITY

'THE COLOUR OF SAYING'

On one occasion when I ran picture exploration as a workshop in a primary school, as we jumped into the picture one girl said, 'I can smell the fireworks.' I asked her to tell me more about the smell. Immediately her brow furrowed as she struggled for words, until eventually she gave up and said, 'Well, it's quite a nice smell.'

But we weren't going to leave it there. I said, 'Pretend you can touch the smell. Do that now and tell me what it feels like.' She said it was soft and fluffy, like cotton wool. Then I suggested that the firework smell had a sound. She told me it was a quiet humming sound. I said, 'Pretend the smell has a colour.' 'It's light purple', she replied, without hesitation. So we agreed that the fireworks had a soft, fluffy, quiet, light purple smell – a far richer and more original description than 'it's quite nice'.

'The colour of saying' is a phrase used by the poet Dylan Thomas to describe the cross-matching of sensory experience in our imaginations. The phenomenon is called synaesthesia and is increasingly regarded as a powerful creative ability that we all possess. Extreme synaesthesics actually hallucinate colours when they hear sounds, or can taste textures through their fingers, etc., but most people do the cross-matching in their imaginations.

Our language is littered with synaesthesic references; for instance the way we associate colours with moods. Encourage students, then, to smell sounds, taste colours, hear textures, and this will enrich their inner life.

Using multisensory visualizations (with synaesthesia as a component if you wish) is a powerful way of developing students' metacognitive skills, developing their ability to internalize their attention and lengthening their concentration span. Also, when students become familiar with the technique they can create their own sensory journeys for each other.

Activity: Format a sensory journey like this:

1 Pretend you have driven your car to the beach. As you prepare to walk down to the sea there is a sudden downpour. Describe the sound of that heavy rain on the roof of the car (Do not use terms like 'pitter-patter', 'drumming', etc.).

2 After the shower you walk barefoot over large rounded pebbles to the sea. Describe the physical sensation of the pebbles on the soles of your feet . . .

3 As you paddle in the shallows you feel something curling around your toes. Describe the shock you felt immediately before you realized it was seaweed. (An ideal opportunity here to ask about the colour of the shock, the taste of the shock, etc.)

4 After paddling you return to the car for a snack. You begin with some strawberries. Describe the taste of strawberries to someone who's never eaten one before, etc.

Sensory journeys can be as short or as extended as you like and set within any context. By having students focus on small, precise descriptive details, mentally and carefully selecting words that vividly convey their impressions, you are helping to improve their writing skills.

Games and Activities: Organizing Information

VISUAL ORGANIZERS

Information that's organized visually (above and beyond lines of writing on a page) is more easily retained and remembered, which is why mind-maps and other visual mapping devices are so powerful. Our subconscious map is a network of associations built up from information that has largely entered through our eyes. Furthermore, visually organized information gives us the whole context, the Big Picture at a glance, and provides great opportunity for us to enrich our understanding by linking details logically.

I began using grid organizers (see Figure 3 opposite) some years ago as part of a creative writing course. Motifs – constituent features that help to define and describe a larger domain – arranged in a 6 × 6 pattern allow us to choose items randomly using a dice (I never say 'die'). My rules for creating such an organizer are:

- use a combination of words and pictures;
- include some motifs that are specific to the topic or area of knowledge;
- include some motifs that are mysterious and ambiguous (the words 'trip' and 'safe', for example).

If you use such a grid in the context of creative writing, suggest to students that in order to generate an idea for a story they use the dice to select two motifs at random. A motif is chosen by rolling the dice twice. Roll it once and count the number along the bottom; roll it again and count upwards – 'along the corridor and up the stairs'. So 4/3 gives us the needle and thread, 2/6 gives us the watch-face, and so on.

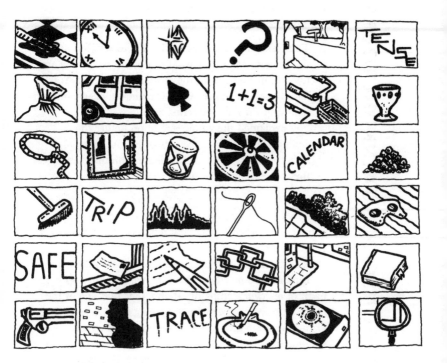

Figure 3: Visual grid organizer

In using 6 × 6 organizers to generate ideas, suggest that two items chosen randomly be put together to make a bigger idea. For the purpose of creative writing, two random items combined will tell us something about the start of the story (when working with younger students I say that the two items can be used in the same sentence). If you set up the task in this way you will have achieved the following:

○ The task is artfully vague, which is to say that the students know exactly what to do, but what they are told about the start of the story is up to them. You have created a structure for learning to occur, but with space for the students' own ideas.

○ You explained the whole operation before the students began. This gives them *pre-processing time*. Subconsciously they will be linking motifs even before they start rolling the dice.

This activity works best when students are in alpha state; when they are not trying hard to make logical connections or work out 'right answers'. Very casually you can suggest that as soon as the second motif is chosen, the idea they make will just pop into their mind.

Linking two motifs in this way helps to develop the habit of *bisociative* thinking. Remember that one of the central aspects of creativity is making novel connections. Using the 6 × 6 grid in this way makes it easy and systematic.

If an idea doesn't spring to mind at once suggest that, like a seed, it will grow into something bigger all by itself and that by next morning it will be clear.

The writer Anaïs Nin once wisely said that we see the world not as it is but as *we are*. Ultimately this is an empowering idea, because we can change the way we are. More of this below; for now let's stay with the notion that we can look at something in many different ways.

On the surface it appears that our 6 × 6 grid in Idea 64 will help students create thriller–spy–murder type stories. But let's suppose we want to write a light romantic comedy instead. Roll the dice twice to select one motif, which will tell you something about the state of the romantic relationship between our two main characters. I rolled 2/2: the letter. The idea that sprang to mind was: *letter – communication at a distance – the two people are rather distant with one another.*

Now let's suppose we want to know something about the fate of this relationship. I rolled 2/5: the car. My first thought was that one of the characters leaves, but then I chose to turn it into a wedding car, so they lived happily ever after (call me old-fashioned if you like).

We could use the same grid – perhaps with minor alterations – to create other kinds of stories. If we said to a group, 'Today we'll use this grid to create a wonderful fantasy story', the students would at once be looking at the grid in a different way, as their perception of it would be filtered through their understanding of what 'fantasy' means.

But the story doesn't end there . . .

Using a 6 × 6 grid offers another strategy for students to consolidate information within any given domain: they can actively engage with its motifs to build larger structures of information.

In the field of creative writing, students become quickly familiar with the motifs of a given genre, and rehearse possible relationships between characters, settings and events. You can suggest that the next item chosen by dice will tell us something about the relationship between the story's hero and a crisis-point in the tale. I rolled 3/5: the ace of spades, and at once thought that the hero gets into trouble in a card-game. In order to know when in the story this happens I simply roll the dice once more – one means at the start of the story, three in the middle, six at the end. I rolled two, so this critical card-game happens a little after the story has opened.

Creating grids for stories the students have studied helps them to become more familiar with the novel's structure. But you can also apply the grid in other subjects. A school I visited in Norwich used a 6 × 6 grid to help Year 2 children learn about the Anglo-Saxons (see Figure 4 opposite). The class teacher took 36 words from the key vocabulary list. The grid was displayed on the wall, so the children always had those motifs in view. We played linking games and even made up stories set in Anglo-Saxon times.

As a creative challenge, consider how you might use the 6 × 6 grid opposite to develop some of the other thinking skills explored in this book.

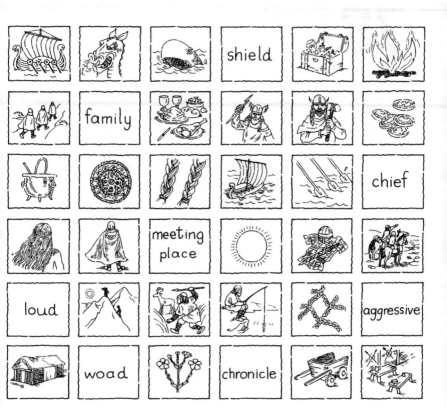

Figure 4: Anglo-Saxon grid

IDEA

78

Most children know the old joke, 'What do you get if you cross a sheep with a kangaroo?' *Answer:* a woolly jumper. But behind the gag is a useful thinking strategy. Criss-Cross is a simple bisociation game that links two ideas at random, either simply to see what emerges or in an endeavour to find new solutions to problems. A bisociation, remember, is the simple linking of two previously unconnected objects, concepts, people, places, etc.

So, for instance, using the 6 × 6 visual grids in Ideas 74 and 77 respectively, let's take an item at random from each and put them together to see what happens. Using dice, I came up with:

A 4/4 a wheel and 1/1 a wooden hut. What comes to mind is a hut on wheels (very eco-friendly), or a hut on a turntable that rotates slowly to follow the sun – how about a greenhouse that turns in the same way?

B 5/2 a street corner and 3/5 a meal on a table. I'm thinking of a corner café, a portable café that sets up in different locations. Now I'm thinking about the street-lamp on the corner . . . How about a tray with a built-in light so you can sit and watch TV in the dark and eat supper at the same time?

C 6/5 a goblet or cup and 6/6 a fire. How about a self-heating cup to keep drinks warm? How about a small container for camping that contains some fuel, firelighters, matches? How about a self-illuminated glass as a fashion item? How about a child's cup that changes colour to tell you when a drink is too hot, or just the right temperature . . . ?

You can of course play Criss-Cross by matching any items. These do not have to be chosen randomly (see also Idea 99: Criss-Cross and the Merlin game).

Earlier I deliberately said 'on the surface' the grid looks like a way of creating thriller–spy–murder stories. But a creative attitude encourages us to look beyond that. Creative exploration presupposes that things are packed with latent meaning, like packages of potential waiting to be unwrapped. Viewed in that light, our grid turns into a wonderful playground of possibilities.

Take, for instance, the motif 6/5 – the cup. First, free-associate whatever comes into your mind that's linked with the idea of 'cup'. Now:

○ Use the PIN strategy: Positive–Interesting–Negative. Use three sheets of paper. On one list the positive aspects of 'cupness'; on another list anything negative. The 'interesting' sheet is for ideas that are neutral or ambiguous, or just for things that don't seem to fit yet in the other two lists.

○ Play the 'Metaphor' game (see Idea 58). The mind is a cup because . . . My life is a cup because . . . The state of the world is a cup because . . .

○ Play the 'Criss-Cross' game. Roll dice to choose two items. So, if you crossed a mirror (2/4) with a book (6/2) you'd get a story that causes you to reflect, or you'd see your own life mirrored in the tale, or you build a mirror into the front cover as a marketing device . . .

○ Use randomly chosen motifs to play the 'Hypothesis' game (see Idea 48). Combine the motifs to create a scenario containing a mystery, then construct hypotheses to explain what's happened.

Thinking creatively at this level makes it easy to use the grid as a problem-solving tool.

Ask your students to identify a problem. This may be a personal difficulty (they won't need to reveal what it is), or a problem in society or the world generally. Now roll the dice to choose a motif, which will reveal something about how that problem will be solved.

Students may gain an immediate insight. If not, suggest that there's no need to try to work out a logical answer. Roll the dice to choose a second motif, which will give a clue about how the first motif will solve the problem.

In other words, go back to the resource – although the true resource of course is the students' own creativity. The motifs on the grid are just prompts.

If insights haven't occurred by now, suggest that by maintaining a clear intention that they will, and it's likely that later on a solution will come to mind clearly.

So, to summarize:

○ the task is artfully vague;
○ by framing the grid as a problem-solver you're filtering your perception of the motifs in light of that goal, and of positive and successful outcomes;
○ before you begin you are already pre-processing the motifs as potential solutions;
○ in seeking a second motif you are thinking bisociatively – and linking two things more than doubles the potential of a motif alone;
○ maintaining intent to create a solution prepares the subconscious creative ground for the seed thought to grow.

If by this time a solution still hasn't come to the students, ask them to use the original motif with the 'Merlin' game in Idea 98. There's always a way forward.

A topic, subject or area of knowledge can be considered as a 'box of motifs' (and at this point I'm tempted to use the PIN technique on that metaphor!). One negative aspect of this is that because certain motifs are conventionally kept in certain boxes, it's usual to try to solve problems within the box. But why? There's nothing to stop us taking a *creative excursion* to other boxes to look for answers.

I heard the story that in the 1970s the technologists at NASA were working on the problem of sending astronauts to Mars. However, politically it became unwise to commit so much money to the project, when social problems at home also needed funding. But the government still wanted to achieve a political coup by sending a US probe to Mars first – but it had to be unmanned, tough and reliable and (relatively) cheap.

So the NASA technologists went to the zoo and talked with the entomologists about insects. They're tough, reliable and successful. How do they work? The NASA people were nosy. They noticed, they asked questions and they returned to their own box with some brilliant insights.

To apply this strategy educationally:

o Prepare a number of small paper circles. On each one write the name of a different topic, subject or area of knowledge.

o Turn them all face-down, except the circle on which is written the name of your topic, which is where the problem exists.

o Turn over one other circle. This is the box you will visit for insights.

THE THREE-COLUMN GAME

This is an extension of the creative excursion idea from Idea 81. Make a three-column matrix as shown in Figure 5 on the next page. The numbering allows you to randomize the motifs you use by rolling two dice together, which gives you a total of between two and 12.

Use one column for motifs – words and/or pictures – from the topic within which the problem exists. Some of these motifs should have a bearing on the problem. Use a second column for motifs from the topic you will visit for insights to solutions. The third column will be 'creatively ambiguous', containing wild-card words and/or images that seem at first to have no link with the problem or its solution.

Incidentally, one way of generating wild-card motifs is to use a picture as a resource. Look again at *The Walker* on p. 68 and notice how I've abstracted motifs from that: the solitary man, the lonely road and the scribbled note. I can use these metaphorically to suggest solutions.

Now define the problem clearly, perhaps in terms of the outcomes you're looking for and/or by breaking it into smaller bits.

Initially work within the 'problem column'. Roll the dice to select two or three motifs and these may in themselves give you insights, or reveal aspects of the problem that you haven't considered.

Next, randomly choose one or two motifs from the 'solution column'. A creative solution might pop into mind instantly. Or treat it as a seed-thought and come back to it later. Finally, you might want to use a wild card to refine the solution or add alternative solutions.

	Problem domain	Solution domain	Wild cards
2			The hurrying figure
3			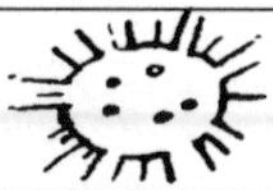
4			The lonely road
5			
6			Hidden corners
7			
8			Discarded rubbish
9			
10			A clutched bag
11			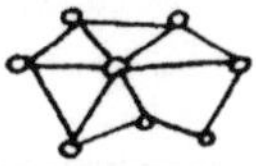
12			Hidden pursuit

Figure 5: The three-column game

TAKING STOCK

We've seen that a creative attitude involves active noticing and questioning. The ground in which these have their roots, and from which the fruits of our thinking grow, are 'the 4Is'.

o *Imagination* The powerful ability to create mental scenarios that we can alter at will, drawing upon the resource of memory and focused on the fixed goal of developing workable solutions.

o *Immersion* Actively engaging with the domain of ideas within which we choose to work: 'stepping into' the field of knowledge so that our exploration and understanding can exist in a multisensory way.

o *Intellectual skills* Our conscious thinking tools, used artfully and deliberately in cognitive space, to create the products, outcomes and final forms of our thinking: our plans realized and applied. But at the outset we need to envision, to contextualize, to apprehend the Big Picture. And to connect the first vision with the final solution requires . . .

o *Intuition* 'Inner tuition', a reliance upon our own subconscious abilities and the art of listening to our own thoughts and feelings, so that we can become more independent and resourceful in our own creativity.

Activity: Perhaps with your students' help, look at a number of topic areas in your subject and discuss how the 4Is could be more fully included.

Games and Activities: Language and Imagination

CONTEXT SENTENCES AND THE SIX BIG IMPORTANT QUESTIONS

Our brains love to contextualize. We talk about the 'need to know', and this is indeed a need that remains unsatisfied until we know enough to make sense of what's going on. Take a sentence like

They shook hands, but only Baxter was smiling.

Most people would find that tantalizing and want to understand what it's all about. It's the kind of sentence that begs further questions. Ask your students to take a minute now to list some that come to mind.

The chances are that most of the questions will fall into six categories: what, where, when, who, how and why. These are the Six Big Important Questions. I'm not telling you anything new, of course. The point I wish to make is that by encouraging this questioning with a low-risk sentence like the one above, and establishing it *as a habit of thought* in your students, then further down the line you can present your groups with more intellectually/creatively challenging information or ideas, and your students will be more likely to ask those Six Big Important Questions than simply be passive recipients of 'facts'.

When I use a context sentence like this I write it out on the board and arrange the students' questions around it by

○ putting different categories of question into different parts of the visual field;
○ colour-coding the categories;
○ highlighting the key (question) words;
○ exploring further by making logical connections between questions.

This establishes the four key principles of mind-mapping.

A connective prompt is a word that encourages a link between two ideas or pieces of information. The word 'because' encourages logical links. I compare 'because' to glue: it sticks two ideas together so that one follows on from the other, or it sticks a reason on to an idea.

You can practise logical linking by playing the 'Because' game. Start with a context sentence such as, 'They shook hands, but only Baxter was smiling.' Explain to the group that when you next say the sentence you'll want a reason *why* they shook hands and/or why Baxter was smiling.

I tend to look for the first hand that goes up in the air, although I know some schools discourage hand-raising. You may listen out for the first response. I want the game to run at a fast pace because I don't want students to be concerned about trying to work out right answers. If a response doesn't follow logically I don't say it's wrong, I say, 'What can we add to make your idea a bit stickier?'

It's important, of course, to insist on appropriate responses.

Playing the 'Because' game is an engaging activity: students want to know 'what happens next' and are interested in the twists and turns of the narrative. A lot of diverse information is generated quickly, so it's ideal as a way in to story-making. More broadly, it acts as a precursor to the language of persuasion and debate, where logic counts.

CONNECTIVE PROMPTING
AND LOGICAL GLUE

'Before' is another useful connective prompt. In this case we're not looking so much for strictly logical links, but rather *chronological* links, going backwards in time.

Referring to our example sentence, when you say 'Before they shook hands . . .' students realize that this is not the start of the narrative: things happened previously that have brought us up to this point. That's an obvious statement to make, but my concern is developing mental flexibility. Even very young children know that a story has a beginning, a middle and an end. And that's how they think about it from the outset, like a forward-pointing arrow. However, that's the finished product. I have never heard a student say that a story has an end, a middle and a beginning – and this is important.

Consciously we think in a linear, logical way. Our spoken and written language reflects this. But subconsciously we survey the map 'all at once together', processing information visually, symbolically, holistically. That's why we go into dreaming phase (see Idea 18) first, to let the Big Picture rise into consciousness.

That said, we have ideas *in any order*. We might envision the end of the story/project first, or a linking piece from the middle. As we plan and realize we need to organize ideas beginning–middle–end, but they don't occur to us like that and so we require the mental dexterity to move backwards and forwards along the linear-sequential line of reasoning.

The 'Before' game helps to achieve this.

'While' is another powerful connective prompt. Start with our example sentence and explain that in the 'While' game, everything happens simultaneously and does not need to be logically connected. However, each 'while' moves further away from the centre. So . . .

- *While they shook hands (but only Baxter was smiling), ten metres away in the flat next door . . .*
- . . . two people were quarrelling.
- *While those two people were quarrelling, a kilometre away in the middle of town . . .*
- . . . shops were closing.
- *While the shops were closing, ten kilometres away on the coast . . .*
- . . . the tide was coming in.

And so on. Notice what's happening. Our attention was initially fixed on a very small detail – they (Baxter and another?) were shaking hands. As the 'While' game progressed we developed an increasingly broader overview which, within a few moments, was ten kilometres in radius.

We have talked of immersion being an important feature of creativity, but the skill of detaching in order to assimilate an overview is vital too. In terms of creative writing it makes the use of the third person conceptually easier to master and creates the mental flexibility to handle 'spatially big' ideas. For students to appreciate the concept of, say, 'the rise and fall of the Roman Empire' they need to be able to think big, spatially and temporally.

Connective prompting helps to develop these abilities.

THE 'IF–THEN' GAME

This is also called the 'Ripple' game. It explores themes, raises issues, connects values and consolidates reasons even if the initial premise is fantastical. When I run the 'If–then' game I usually want it to proceed at a more leisurely pace than the 'Because' game, underlining the principle that consequences need to be considered. The activity might run as follows:

○ TEACHER: *If people's thoughts appeared in bubbles above their heads, then . . .*
○ STUDENTS: You'd have to be really careful about what you thought!
○ *And if you needed to be so careful, then . . .*
○ Some people would sit around thinking all day and never do anything.
○ *And if some people never did anything, then . . .*
○ The people who didn't care if their thoughts were seen would be more active – they'd have all the fun.
○ *And if those people had all the fun, then . . .*
○ They'd get the most done.
○ *What can we say to make that reason a bit stickier? They'd get the most done because . . .*
○ They'd get the most done because they wouldn't worry about other people seeing their thoughts.
○ *OK, good –*
○ And because they're getting the most done they'd be happiest, so their thoughts would look nicer anyway.
○ *And if their thoughts looked nicer anyway, then . . .*

And so on. The 'If–then' game is a standard tool in the development of philosophical thinking in students, where the SAT strategy is used – Sitting and Thinking/Talking (as opposed to the GAS strategy for scientific/technical questions – Go And See).

Being nosy by questioning lies at the heart of creativity in learning. 'Quality questioning' implies an understanding of different types of questions and the purposes for which they are asked, plus the deliberate consideration of the criteria of their quality.

Basic categories of questions include:

○ *Philosophical or scientific/technical?* Philosophical questions are not so much answered as explored through the SAT strategy. Scientific/technical questions can be methodically investigated and often answered through the GAS strategy (see Idea 90).
○ *Closed or open?* Closed questions are convergent and lead towards a particular answer. Open questions are divergent and throw up more information and further questions.
○ *Small-scale or large-scale?* This refers to the scale of exploration across a domain of knowledge.

Other criteria of value include:

○ *Relevance* How closely linked is the question to the area of enquiry and my needs?
○ *Inclusiveness* How far does the question use what I already know?
○ *Breadth and depth* How much useful information will the answer give me?
○ *Flexibility* How many ways can I think about or use the answer?
○ *Incisiveness* How many questions does the answer give me? How many further questions are generated?
○ *Learning* How much does the answer increase my understanding? How much more information now makes greater sense?
○ *Resonance/insight* How much does the answer *feel* right to me? How does it connect with what I already know to be true?
○ *Challenge* How deeply does the answer lead me to question, doubt and test my understanding?

Activity: With your students, make a list of questions pertinent to your subject area and study them with the above criteria in mind.

This simple activity encourages students to reflect on and refine their questions within any topic area. You can set it up as a 'mind game' where the computer is imaginary or (and this adds fun for younger children) actually have a gift-wrapped box on display. This is how the game works:

○ Say to the students: 'In this box is the cleverest computer in the world. It's linked to the Internet so it can find information very quickly. If you could ask the computer any questions, what would they be?' Have the students write their questions down and, if there's time, pick a few and discuss why those students would ask them. Continue . . .

○ 'However, this computer will only answer questions that you don't already know the answers to.' This encourages students to move outside their comfort-zone.

○ 'And because this is a computer, it will only answer questions that are absolutely clear in their meaning [i.e. unambiguous].' Give an example, such as 'How could I get rich?' Discuss what 'rich' can mean. Rich compared to whom? How would you decide that you were rich?, etc. Students might now want to refine their lists further, but you'll still have a long class-list of questions. Now say . . .

○ 'The computer uses a lot of power and its batteries are low. It can only answer three of the questions we have left. How will we decide which ones to ask?' This encourages discussion of the criteria of quality for questions (see Idea 89 for tips).

When you have a short-list of three quality questions, discuss ways of helping the computer to find out the answers.

This simple strategy usually throws up some fascinating (and sometimes unnerving) insights about what we think we know. It also quickly leads to fruitful discussion of what words can mean and philosophical enquiry into what knowledge is and how we know what we know (these days this is called cognitive science and, previously, epistemology).

The idea is simply to pretend that one doesn't know anything about the topic in question. You can set up the session with both yourself and the students in this state, or you might just have the students playing the game of pretend. Alternatively, split the class into two groups – the enquirers who know nothing and the 'experts' who will endeavour to offer answers and explanations.

You can introduce the game by looking around the classroom and kicking off with a few questions such as

○ I wonder why that's called a window?
○ How is glass made?
○ When was the idea of glass first thought of?
○ If something in nature first gave people the idea for making glass, what might it have been?
○ What does the word 'glass' mean anyway?

(As these questions came to me I realized how frighteningly little I knew about the subject!)

It has been said that a good teacher is never afraid to admit 'I don't know – but how might we find out?' This game can be an object-lesson for those of us who base our authority as teachers on what we (think we) know. It also of course highlights the power and importance of enquiry as a learning behaviour, and rehearses the kinds of questions that move us away from the state of ignorance towards that of understanding.

LET'S PRETEND WE DON'T KNOW ANYTHING

I still clearly recall a teacher who came along to one of my presentations. He approached me during coffee and said, 'I decided to learn more about creative thinking because of what happened a couple of weeks ago. I was discussing an aspect of social geography with my Year 10 students and at one point I said, "And what do you think about this issue?" One boy replied – with no trace of irony – "I don't know sir. What *do* I think?" This was one of the academically more able students in the group and yet here he was with no view on the issue and leaning on me to offer him some predigested opinion. I was horrified.'

Many years ago the educationalists Neil Postman and Charles Weingartner (in their superb book *Teaching as a Subversive Activity*) suggest chillingly that 'Students enter schools as question-marks and leave as full-stops.' Part of our role as educators must surely be to have students leave our care as question-marks, armed with strategies for finding useful answers.

Introduce the 'Lesson of Questions' strategy by saying to your group, 'Today we are studying xxx. After this statement I will only respond to you by asking questions that you can respond to with what you think are answers, or with more questions . . .'

And then let the lesson take its course. You may experience an almost overwhelming desire to supply answers – resist that and be true to your resolve. When the strategy is successful, the students will have learned to think a little more for themselves and be more assured in selecting the kinds of questions that move their enquiry forward.

Actively asking quality questions counters the tendency for students to be simply passive recipients of facts. It is, of course, true that they need to absorb huge amounts of relevant information before they can ask *informed* questions – perhaps we've all met the child who habitually asks 'why?' in a vacuous way without much desire to have his or her curiosity satisfied. There are few more irritating individuals.

'(W)ringing the changes' is a creative thinking game which encourages the manipulation of ideas and can generate 'why' at any point – although by now students will have other tools to help them find answers: logical linking, cause–effect relationships, criteria of quality, etc.

I often begin using this game in the context of story-making with younger children. Start with a familiar story-based idea and encourage students to take the motifs it contains and spin them off in various ways.

The three little pigs were friends.

- The three pigs were not friends.
- Two pigs were friends, but not friends with the third pig.
- The big bad wolf was a friend of one of the pigs.
- The wolf hated the third pig.
- The pig that the wolf hated was best friends with another pig.

And so on. Notice how this game creates opportunities for other activities we've already explored.

At a more sophisticated level, using factual information, '(W)ringing the changes' throws up wrong or nonsensical ideas: the challenge is to question and explore why they are wrong. For example, what nonsensical ideas would spin off from

The Moon goes around the Earth. The Earth goes around the Sun.

Like many of the other activities we've touched upon, this game can be fun to play. It requires quick thinking and noticing the ideas that rise spontaneously to mind. Start with a context sentence such as:

Jones lay slumped on the sofa.

○ *And fortunately?*
He was catching up on sleep.
○ *But unfortunately?*
His lighted cigarette had caused the sofa to catch fire.
○ *The sofa caught fire. And fortunately?*
Jones smelt the smoke and woke up.
○ *But unfortunately?*
The smoke was so thick he couldn't find the door.
○ *He couldn't find the door. And fortunately?*
A neighbour smelt the smoke, hurried round and opened the door.
○ *But unfortunately?*
He was overcome by the smoke and passed out.

And so on.

Like the 'Because' game and others, the 'Fortunately/ unfortunately' game generates lots of ideas and explores issues quickly. It also, most importantly, encourages a mental habit called 'flipping the coin', which means looking at two sides of an idea, issue or situation simultaneously. This mental faculty becomes useful in the language of discussion, debate and persuasion, where we need to anticipate and appreciate opposing viewpoints. It can also develop into a life-skill. We wonder whether someone 'sees the glass half-full or half-empty': is a person an optimist or a pessimist? The fact is, we can have the mental flexibility to see both perspectives at once, and then to choose which position we'll adopt, thereby gaining more control over our emotional response.

Acronyms are words formed from the first letters of other words. 'Acronym' itself comes from the Greek *akron*, meaning 'end', together with *-onum = onoma*, name.

Ideas 117 and 118 give examples of acronyms that are real words in themselves, and which in these cases highlight an attitude. Some acronyms such as and laser only came to be regarded as words after a period of time, when they had been absorbed into the language. Many people don't even realize that 'laser' is an acronym – Light Amplification by Stimulated Emission of Radiation. To know the acronym is also to gain an insight into how a laser works.

Making up new acronyms is a creative way of focusing students' attention on a chosen topic and can lead to a greater sense of authority and self-confidence when talking about it. When students create their own acronyms they are more likely to remember what they refer to. Making acronyms also encourages students to 'reach for the right words' and keep to the point.

Activity: Play with words such as LEARN, IDEA, STORY. From the many suggestions the class is likely to generate, decide together which combination of qualities makes for the most accurate or effective acronym.

Mnemonics are devices to aid recollection. The word comes from the Greek *mnemonikos*, out of *mnemon*, mindful. As a young boy I first remembered the order of the planets outward from the Sun by learning that 'Many Volcanoes Erupt Mulberry Jam Sandwiches Under Normal Pressure' (Mercury – Venus – Earth – Mars – Jupiter – Saturn – Uranus – Neptune – Pluto). And most people know that 'Richard Of York Gained Battles In Vain' (Red – Orange – Yellow – Green – Blue – Indigo – Violet, the order of colours in the visible part of the spectrum).

Mnemonics work because they are often funny or wacky and because they exploit the structure of sentences, which is embedded in our brains from an early age (and may even be innate). Learning a mnemonic is generally easier than learning the list of items it refers to. Making up mnemonics combines the benefits of clearer recollection with the fun of creativity.

So: My Vicious Eel Makes Journeys So Underwear Needn't Pinch.

Or: Robert, Oh Yesterday Guzzled Beer In Vats.

It's in dispute whether Pluto can actually be defined as a planet, so why not flex your creative muscles by inventing a new mnemonic that just takes us up to Neptune?

These short pithy sayings are strewn throughout our language. Sometimes they convey great wisdom – Youth lives on hope, old age on remembrance. Sometimes they seem to limit possibilities – You cannot teach an old dog new tricks. Now and again their meaning seems obscure – Who will bell the cat? Once in a while they are just plain wrong – Silence gives consent. Playing with proverbs is an easy and enjoyable way of rehearsing a variety of creative strategies.

Activity:

○ Have students suggest possible explanations for obscure or ambiguous proverbs – Much cry, little wool.

○ Suggest likely scenarios that prove the wisdom of proverbs – Old wounds soon bleed.

○ Use proverbs as themes for stories – There are none so blind as those who will not see.

○ Use proverbs as discussion/debating points – The public pays with ingratitude.

○ Make up new proverbs that restate the meanings of established ones – Stir up not a hornet's nest. (Disturb not teachers in the staffroom at break-time!)

○ Explain proverbs in down-to-earth language to highlight their metaphorical nature – There are many ways to skin a cat (there are many possible strategies for solving a problem).

○ Play the 'What if?' game (Idea 105) to explore the truth of proverbs – what if the end always does justify the means?

○ Ask the Six Big Important Questions (Idea 84) to explore proverbs further – Knowledge is power. (When is this true? When not true? What examples can we think of? Who seems to embody that belief? How does this idea apply in science, in politics, in daily life?)

PLAYING WITH PROVERBS

In this case Merlin is the wizard of our own creative imagination. With a wave of a wand we can transform the way we look at something. The 'Merlin' game itself is a fruitful, robust and focused brainstorm.

o Select a problem.
o State your fixed goal.
o Identify the components you have to work with.

The 'Merlin' game generates possible strategies for solution. So, for example:

o I'm a chocolate-maker and I'm not selling enough chocolate.
o I intend to increase my sales.
o The components I have to work with are: the chocolate itself and its ingredients; the wrappings; an advertising campaign; an advertising budget.

Then you brainstorm with these components in the following ways:

o enlarge something
o reduce
o stretch
o eliminate
o substitute
o reverse.

Be aware that this game works within the dreamer phase of the Disney Strategy (see Idea 18). We are envisioning possibilities rather than entering the realist phase to ask how these ideas could be planned and realized. As with more basic brainstorming techniques, all ideas are valued because they all have potential.

You can use the 'Merlin' game for story-making. With younger students I change the vocabulary:

o make bigger
o make smaller
o change the shape of something
o take something away
o swap something
o turn something around.

The Merlin Game, as outlined in the previous idea, is always creative in that it encourages us to examine ideas from many perspectives. Combining the strategy with the outcomes of the Criss-Cross game (see Idea 78) throws up many further possibilities.

Motifs that emerged from the Criss-Cross game were a goblet and fire. Applying the Merlin strategy we get:

○ *Enlarge* Roadways composed of a material that soaks up heat in the day and radiates at night, keeping the surface ice free in winter.
○ *Reduce* Decorative lapel badges acting as tiny solar cells to power personal attack alarms, hearing aids, personal stereos, etc.
○ *Stretch* Heat-absorbent clothing to keep people warm for nothing.
○ *Eliminate* A substance like flexible plastic that can be moulded to any shape, and when it's heated it hardens to retain that shape.
○ *Substitute* Solid for liquid, so we get self-illuminating paint or a gel that stores heat.
○ *Reverse* How about 'anti-glass' that actively soaks up light and darkens a room?

Activity: Use dice with the grids from Ideas 74 and 77 to choose two motifs at random. How might they combine? When you have some ideas to play with, apply the Merlin technique and see what happens.

THE PYRAMID ORGANIZER

Another powerful visual organizer is the pyramid shape. This immediately puts the idea of depth and 'layeredness' in front of the eye and suggests a hierarchical structure. In terms of a creative attitude, we can envisage a pyramid split into three divisions. The bottom layer represents the fundamental aspects of creativity itself – curiosity, noticing, asking, linking and multiple viewpoints. The bulk of the rest of the pyramid would be filled with activities such as those in this book, arranged into strategies leading towards the peak, which is the fixed goal of allowing our students to be independent creative thinkers.

Another use for the organizer is to create two layers. The tip of the pyramid (allowing enough room to write one statement) represents the *surface structure* – what we are told. The rest of the pyramid suggests a *deep structure*, within which creative exploration could occur. As an example, suppose in the surface structure box I wrote, 'A can of fizzy drink'. The rest of the organizer would arrange my exploration of that idea. What is the drink made of? How are those ingredients obtained? Why is that drink so popular? How is the can made? What happens to it after I've finished with it?

Using the same version of the organizer, in the surface structure box I write, 'They shook hands, but only Baxter was smiling.' The rest of the box would be filled up with the outcomes of my thinking about that statement; what I deduce, infer, assume, speculate about, examples of answers to the Six Big Important Questions, logical linking, etc.

People are like onions: they can make you cry, and they have layers. Figure 6 (p.119) illustrates how a pyramid organizer can make the depth and layeredness of people explicit for students.

○ *Basic identifiers* refers to the two or three details by which a character might be introduced into a story or 'tagged' in the memory; so name, age, a physical detail, etc.

○ *One special detail* is a vivid particularity (see Idea 111), something which makes that person special or unique. Such a detail might be drawn from any layer of the individual.

○ *Personality* – thoughts, feelings, traits, behaviours – helps to create someone's physical appearance. As students reflect on a character that they've learned about, met in a story or want to create for themselves, the organizer carries the message that to judge a book by its cover is simplistic and underestimates the depth and complexity of human beings.

○ *Background* Similarly, past experiences help to shape personality. Causes have effects and consequences. Giving thought to this layer of the pyramid leads towards greater understanding and empathy.

○ *Possible futures* What we make of ourselves rests on how we envisage the future. Future-mapping – considering possible futures – is for me the bedrock on which an individual stands in the world. I'm emphatically not talking about 'dwelling in the future' or wishful thinking. Future-mapping draws upon my past experience and focuses on the decisions I make now and clarifies my goals for tomorrow.

○ *Feelings and motivations* – these are what move us through life, our thoughts translated into actions. At the deepest level, feelings and motivations are linked to spirituality in Robert Dilts' neurological levels model of human behaviour (see Idea 29).

THE KNOWLEDGE PYRAMID

The pyramid organizer can also be used to allow students to retain and remember factual information more clearly. Normally such information is arranged in notebooks as lines of writing interspersed with pictures, diagrams, graphs, etc. Writing in the pyramid with diagrams arranged around the outside is more memorable. Construct the organizer thus, from the top downwards:

o At the peak is a 'gee whizz' idea. This is the doorway into the domain of knowledge.

o Next are key ideas and principles, simply stated. Albert Einstein maintained that things should be kept as simple as possible, but no simpler. This layer outlines the frame within which further learning takes place.

o Elaboration of key ideas follows. In this box the bigger ideas are split into smaller parts and explored further. Note that there's not much room in these boxes, so words have to be carefully chosen and each one must count.

o Next is supplementary information. This can include links with other topic areas and links with the students' own lives, giving them the opportunity to 'humanize the knowledge'.

o The bottom layer, on which the structure of learning is built, contains the outcomes of the students' thinking about the knowledge. Their ideas resulting from some of the activities in this book would be written here.

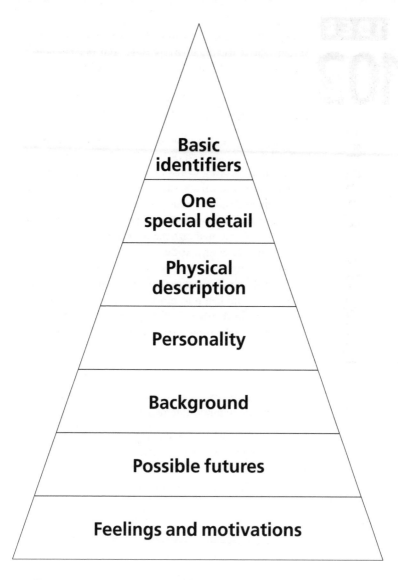

Figure 6: Pyramid organizer for character

The pyramid organizer also makes explicit the structure of journalistic writing and reportage. For this purpose the pyramid would be split into the following layers:

○ *Headline* At the tip of the pyramid create a box that's big enough for a few well-chosen words. These need to 'hook the eye' and catch the reader's attention at once. In more sensationalist newspapers, headlines tend to be composed of *lexical words*, the main meaning-carrying words of a sentence, while *grammatical words* are left out; these are words which specify and modify meaning but carry relatively little meaning of their own. So in 'The cat sat on the mat', 'cat', 'sat' and 'mat' are the lexical words while 'the' and 'on' are grammatical.

○ *Byline* In this box there is space to write one or two well-constructed sentences which elucidate the headline and begin to move the story on.

○ *Key facts* In this box there is room to write a short paragraph which outlines the main features of the story.

○ *Supplementary information* This adds detail to the key facts.

○ The bottom box often rounds off the story with quotes, eyewitness statements, opinions, etc.

Incidentally, when a newspaper story is edited for space, the editor will work from the bottom upwards. This is why newspaper stories sometimes consist only of a headline, byline and brief paragraph.

Stories are powerful. They are engaging and entertaining. They embody a process of moving towards a satisfactory conclusion – in other words, they are dynamic rather than static. They contain embedded metaphors and often 'lessons for life', scripts and subtexts which unfold strategies for dealing with problems. Stories may also use conventional structures, themes and motifs to go beyond the conventional into new territory.

I have mentioned elsewhere how the narrative-dynamic model for learning can be used as an alternative strategy to the traditional model of objectives–content–methodology–evaluation (see Idea 50). At this stage let me add some more details (see Figure 7, p. 122).

○ Pre-processing allows students to draw together ideas that they think relate to the new learning you want them to do. If I'm starting a topic on Monday, I'll mention it on Friday so that students have pre-processing time before we connect things already learned to new information.

○ 'Gee whizz facts'. A story needs a strong opening, as does a lesson. A fact or idea with a 'wow' factor acts as a tempting doorway into the domain of new knowledge.

○ A problem posed within the domain initiates a process of exploration and allows students to become adventurers with you as their guide.

○ Knowledge emerges out of human endeavour. Ideas come from human minds. Humanizing the knowledge 'includes the knower in the known' in two ways: it mentions the people behind the ideas, and it creates a human link between the knowledge and the learner.

○ Vivid particularities (see Idea 111) continue to immerse and engage the learners.

○ Value it as well as evaluate.

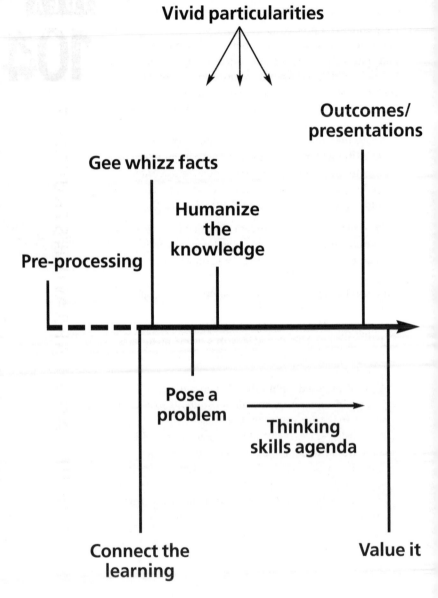

Figure 7: Narrative-dynamic model for teaching and learning

It has been said that the whole of science fiction is predicated on the words 'what if'. Those same words can launch creative explorations into realms of factual knowledge, incorporating many of the activities we've already looked at. 'What if . . .?' frames a question that is often large-scale and divergent, but may be philosophical or scientific/technical. Working on the principle of 'to have good ideas you need to have many ideas', this game uses the question to kickstart freely associative brainstorming – although these three sub-questions are usefully appended:

○ What could the world be like?
○ What problems might we face?
○ How will we solve those problems? (Notice the presupposition of success – 'will' – embedded in the final question.)

One value of the game is that it allows students to explore real themes and issues, solve real problems and engage with real knowledge in any given domain. Even if the initial scenario is fantastical, these things could happen.

One of my favourite 'what ifs' is: *What if gravity switched off unexpectedly for five minutes each day?* This leads to discussions about: the nature of gravity; mass, inertia, orbits and trajectories; and technical difficulties aboard manned spacecraft. One student proposed the Velcro suit as a way of preventing people from floating away. The 'eyes' of the Velcro were incorporated into the walls of buildings, etc.

Another benefit of the game is that once students become familiar with it, they can be encouraged to invent their own 'what if?' examples as a creative challenge.

IDEA

105

THE 'WHAT IF?' GAME

'WHAT IF?' STARS

'What if?' stars extend the basic game and focus questioning and attention into smaller scales of detail.

Another enjoyable 'what if?' activity is, 'What if, when adults had completed their families, the adults began to shrink – so that by the time people were 70 years old they were only one inch tall?' Again this is a fantastical notion, but it produced some useful and fascinating ideas . . .

One group decided that radio-controlled mini helicopters could be used to take tiny older people to the supermarket. There would need to be an ageist employment policy for door staff; they'd need to be big, therefore younger, to scare away any cats or dogs hanging around the supermarket to eat the mice-sized pensioners. Items that older people wanted to buy would have to be put close to the floor. There'd need to be small ramps and elevators up to higher shelves. Baked beans would need to be individually canned for very old people who were so small they could only eat one bean with their breakfast . . .

In one sense the students' creativity is already being focused into making provision for minority (different-sized) groups in society. 'What if?' stars bring ideas to the point.

Draw a large five- or six-pointed star and write the 'What if?' question in the centre. At each point of the star write the area in which brainstorming will focus. So, using the example above, I might put at the points of the star: supermarket design, transport, schooling, medical provision and house design.

Although 'what if?' is a divergent question that opens up the exploration of ideas, it need not be an excuse for students' imaginations to run away with them. Creativity, remember, is not chaos: creative energy can be controlled and directed. The basic 'What if?' game can be modified to focus students' thinking along particular lines:

○ Use 'what if?' within particular subject or topic areas. Asking 'What if dinosaurs never became extinct?' opens up discussion of evolution, food-chains, habitats, ethical questions concerning humanity's 'management' of the natural world, etc. All the while students are manipulating information and meaningfully rehearsing the concepts you want them to understand.

○ Combine 'what if?' questions with the Merlin game (Idea 98). So what if gravity on Earth were different?
  – What if it was 50 per cent stronger?
  – What if it was 50 per cent weaker?
  – What if gravitational pull varied noticeably with height?
  – What if gravity disappeared entirely for short periods?
  – What if gravity changed according to the Moon's phases?
  – What if a repulsive force (anti-gravity) suddenly took the place of gravity?

○ Use a 'what if?' star to direct thinking. Draw a five-point star and put a topic heading at each point, for example school, transport, food production, etc. Now use one of the 'what if?' scenarios above. So, what if gravity disappeared entirely for short periods: what problems would we encounter at school, with transport . . . How will we solve such problems?

THE 'WHY?' GAME

As I was running the 'What if?' game with a class, at one point a student said, 'But why *aren't* humans only one inch tall? Why do we usually grow to several feet?' This is a pertinent question, and it led to several others including:

o Why are animals and plants such different sizes?
o Why do we stop growing in adulthood?
o How do creatures know when to stop growing?
o Is there a limit to the size a creature can grow?
o Is a huge patch of mould one plant or many?

The 'What if?' game leads naturally to the 'Why?' game, which offers a rich field for creative thinking and incorporates many of the thinking tools we've explored in this book. Young children, it has been said, have the wonderful capability to create 'naïve theories of everything'. They make up fantastical stories to explain the mysterious world around them in order to satisfy their basic need to know. At a more sophisticated level, hypotheses in many fields of enquiry perform the same function. The scientific method rests on the 'Why?' game, where the question 'why?' leads to a number of hypotheses, which are tested against evidence gained through investigation. When theories grow out of hypothesis and experiment, the 'positive pressure' to find evidence and counter-evidence continues to drive the enquiry. This is how knowledge and understanding evolve.

Put a 'why?' question on your classroom wall each day, and see what happens.

Young children tend to see the world in extremes. People are tall or short, fat or thin, happy or sad. Usually as we grow we realize that between such extremes lies a huge range of variation: we mediate our understanding by deciding where 'along the line' we stand. Failure to do this leads to naïvety, cognitive distortion and extremism.

'Mediation' comes from the Latin for 'middle' or 'to be in the middle'. Mediation in any sense presupposes an understanding of variety between extremes and a range of possible standpoints. Here are a couple of ideas for developing students' understanding of this.

MEDIATIONS

○ Referring to the character pyramid in Idea 101 (Figure 6, p. 119), make a vertical list of traits and qualities: tallness, attractiveness, selfishness, popularity, ambition, and so on. Beside each word draw a horizontal line so that you end up with a stack of such lines. Above the stack do a number-line 1–6.

Now instead of asking, 'Is this person tall or short?' (bipolar thinking), you can ask, 'How tall is this person?' and mediate your answer by making a mark along the line. The 1–6 numbering also gives you the option of using a dice to generate random answers. This leads to some fascinating character profiles!

○ The 'three perceptual positions' are sometimes used in mediation to resolve conflict. Positions A and B represent the polarized viewpoints of the quarrellers. Position C is that of the 'neutral observer'. Imagine a line drawn between A and B. C invites each quarreller in turn to make a statement that would result in taking a small step towards the middle. When they are close enough, they can shake hands!

The circle is another powerful way of organizing information visually. We'll see how it can be used to evaluate creative work in Idea 114, but before that . . .

o Create a circle and fill it with words and pictures. This is quickly and easily done on the computer. Using Word you can import Clip Art and position words with WordArt. Alternatively, draw on paper and cut out pictures and words from magazines and newspapers. These can be chosen randomly, although make some of the words and pictures ambiguous.

When the circle is filled, say to the group, 'Pretend these are thoughts going on inside a person's mind. Why is he or she thinking about these things, and why is he or she thinking of them *in this way*?' The first part of the question invites speculation, while the second part encourages interpretation. One immediate outcome of this activity is that students realize we can look at the same thing but all see something quite different.

o *Plot arcing* Instead of thinking of a story along a line, bend the line around into a circle that doesn't quite join up. Pick two points on the circle, say point A and point B. Something that happens at A will have consequences at B – although at the moment we don't know what.

Take a coin and begin to ask questions about A that can be answered yes or no. Flip the coin for the answer – heads means yes, tails means no. When you know what's happening at point A, decide what's going on at B.

Bringing it all Together

Traditionally, the creative power of ideas has been judged on their originality and usefulness. This is to some extent a controversial notion, since creativity in learners is an attitude; besides which the creative power and value of an idea might not be fully apparent at the time, but may emerge later. However, here are some guidelines that you and your students might find useful:

o *Conventions of genre and form* The extent of understanding in any area is partly determined by the elegance with which students use the vocabulary of that domain, subject or topic. Giving motifs their conventional meaning in that domain and expressing that knowledge, according to the conventions of correct speech and writing, demonstrates understanding. Extraneous motifs and unconventional expression of them suggests lack of understanding – although in rare cases hints at genius!

o *Affective response* This aspect is concerned with the 'emotional content' of creative work. A creative attitude presupposes a sense of curiosity and wonder. Also, any powerful communication of an idea is one where the emotional response intended by the creator is matched by that of the 'consumer'. One instance is if, as a writer, I intend readers to be chilled by my ghost-story *and they are*, then intention and effect are congruent, which is a measure of the power of the idea.

o *Vivid particularities* Ideas, or statements expressing ideas, which create a vivid mental image and make a strong emotional impact. The 'soft, fluffy, quiet, light purple smell of the fireworks' (see Idea 72) is a good example.

o *Technical accuracy* – in terms of written outcomes and conventional understanding of ideas.

Simply put, in commenting on a student's work, look for three points you can praise, followed by one point for improvement. This evokes the powerful *pattern of three*. If you tell a student he or she has done something well, he or she can put it down to chance. Pick out two things done well and it can be attributed to coincidence. But when you've identified three things, the weight of evidence is harder to deny and the student is more likely to be convinced they've done well. By 'catching them doing something right' three times and telling them, you've also cushioned them so that the point you pick for further improvement doesn't feel like negative criticism.

I've also seen this technique used with younger children, where it's often called 'three stars and a wish'. When children are accustomed to the teacher's use of the 3:1 ratio they can use it for themselves. Give each child three gold stars for them to put on their work, in the margin beside the good idea, or at the end where the child can write/draw about what he or she has done well. Then have the child draw an upward-pointing arrow, at the top of which a note is made of how improvement in the fourth thing will be made.

THE 3:1 RATIO FOR FEEDBACK

Have you heard about the young child during his first week in Year 3 who answered all of the questions in a maths exercise incorrectly? After his teacher handed the marked work back to him he beamed and said 'Now I know you love me very much. You've given me all these kisses.'

The marks we make on students' work can have a powerful influence on their attitude, confidence and beliefs about their own learning. Because of the politically imposed nature of our educational system, much of the marking that teachers do is corrective and some of it is negative. Perhaps this is inevitable given the current climate, but I suggest that we can enrich the way we mark to reflect the ethos of the creative thinking approach to learning that I have advocated throughout this book.

Activity: Here are some icons that you might find useful to incorporate into your marking regime, followed by a few others for you to play with creatively.

Although the icons here are stylized, it's an advantage of course if they are quick and easy to draw! Feel free to modify and add to this list as you wish.

Symbol	Intended meaning	Useful modifications
 ↗ (three-way arrow)	What other ideas/ strategies/alternatives/ solutions can you think of?	
 ↺ (looping arrow)	Go back and look again to see what else you can discover.	
 →←	Think about the opposite viewpoint.	
 》》》	Show the details of your argument more clearly.	
 (puzzle piece)	Put some more clues/ details of your reasoning into your work.	
OP	This is an opinion. It's not backed up by reasons.	
OP✓	You've given reasons for your opinion. Well done.	
 (magnifying glass)	Examine your argument/reasoning/ conclusions in more detail.	
 (magic wand)	Apply the Merlin Strategy. +E – Enlarge, etc.	
 (light bulb with !)	Good idea.	

Figure 8: New marking symbols

Creativity both encourages and develops 'higher-order thinking', to use Howard Bloom's terminology. Currently the emphasis of the curriculum seems to be on the lower levels of Bloom's hierarchy: knowledge and comprehension. Although at worst 'comprehension' can mean students simply parroting the notes in their notebooks, or reiterating more or less verbatim the ideas of others or working without insight to create the *appearance* of comprehension (how well I remember getting the right answers to maths problems without really understanding how I did it).

You can assess students' levels of thinking – and guide them into doing it for themselves – by creating a circle organizer, as shown in Figure 9. Each segment of the organizer can focus on a different subject, topics or ideas within one subject area.

Assess the level of thinking by making a mark in each segment using Bloom's terminology and the criteria below. The closer each mark is to the edge of the circle, the higher the level of thinking.

1 *Knowledge* I can recall/remember something previously learned.
2 *Comprehension* I have a basic understanding. I can explain the idea in my own words.
3 *Application* I can use the knowledge/idea/skill in a different way.
4 *Analysis* I can see how and why different ideas fit together. When ideas don't work together, I can explain why.
5 *Evaluation* I can use the ideas to decide how to judge something.
6 *Synthesis* I can put lots of ideas together to make something new.

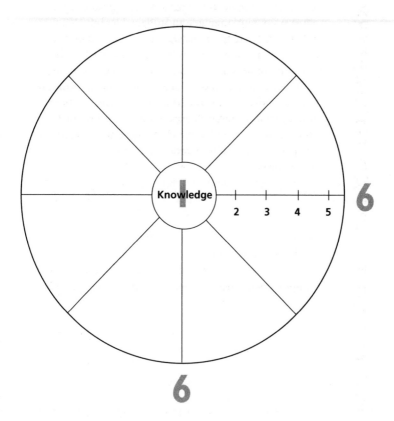

Figure 9: Circle organizer for assessing understanding

WALKING ALONG THE ROAD TO MASTERY

We all know about the *learning curve*, although I prefer to think of the learning process as 'walking along the road to mastery'. When I work with students I know that I've already walked a long way down that road. What I don't want to do is shout to them from where I am. Nor am I interested in 'pushing', 'pulling' or 'stretching' them (or any other example of the terminology of torture that's often used with reference to students' learning). I want to walk with them – to paraphrase George Bernard Shaw – as a fellow traveller of whom they asked the way. I point ahead: ahead of myself as well as of them.

If we continue to walk in an environment of mutual respect, where curiosity and ideas are valued, where mistakes are counted as experience, we evolve into a state of mastery, where the skills we've been practising are performed to a high order of complexity and effectiveness.

Activity: Discuss the idea of a learning curve with your students. Suggest other metaphors such as a road, a flowing river or a growing garden. Develop these metaphors in a helpful way. For instance, if we were gardeners how could we help each other to make the garden grow? If we were all travellers on the road, what signposts could we put up to help people who followed after us?

'Authenticity' has roots in several languages and links with 'to commit and effect', 'to master', 'to accomplish' and 'to gain'. It expresses itself as a positive energy that helps to drive the learning process when:

O Tasks are set which are relevant to the real world, in so far as students can personalize their relationship to them and work meaningfully towards workable solutions.

O Learners are given responsibility ('the ability to respond') and opportunities to do so in thinking for themselves and organizing themselves, with encouragement towards greater self-confidence.

O When both teachers and learners encourage real accountability in setting and maintaining high standards and effective outcomes. 'Real' in this sense comes about through adherence to the ethos of creativity, through discussion, collaboration, mutual respect and agreement.

Creative thinkers can have IDEAS NOW because they are:

- o **I**nquisitive
- o **D**aydreamy
- o **E**xcited
- o **A**ttentive
- o **S**ensitive

- o **N**osy
- o **O**n-the-ball
- o **W**ondering

o   *Connect* – link ideas, create the Big Picture.
o   *Relate* – personalize the knowledge, actively seek its relevance in your life.
o   *Explore* – be nosy, notice, question and seek solutions.
o   *Analyse* – step back and evaluate (and value it!), having envisioned, go into realist and critic phases (see Idea 18).
o   *Transform* – use creative insights to build further ideas and strategies. One idea makes lots of ideas.
o   *Experience* – enjoy the journey.

SO – CREATE!

RECOGNIZING EFFECTIVE LEARNERS

Accelerated learning books often talk about students 'learning how to learn'. For me this is what a creative attitude is all about. As we near the end of our exploration together, let's summarize how that attitude leads to effective learning ability.

○ Effectives learners come to see themselves and others differently.
○ They accept themselves and their feelings more completely, but work more capably towards developing a sense of 'response-ability'.
○ They become more independent and self-directing.
○ They become more flexible in their perceptions and more considered in their judgements.
○ They adopt realistic goals that are congruent with their increasing capabilities.

The purpose of the curriculum is not to cover but to uncover.
Anon.

Nothing in education is more astonishing as the amount of ignorance it accumulates in the form of inert facts.
Henry Brook Adams

The moment one definitely commits oneself, then Providence moves too.
Goethe

Chop your own wood and it will warm you twice.
Traditional saying

The 'silly' question is the first intimation of some totally new development.
Alfred North Whitehead

In the long history of human and animal kind, those who have learned to improvise most effectively have prevailed.
Charles Darwin

The only effective method of education is to be an example.
Albert Einstein

Work on deepening the moment.
Patrice Baldwin

Get your facts first and then you can distort them as much as you like.
Mark Twain

It is the supreme art of the teacher to awaken joy in creative expression and knowledge.
Albert Einstein

IDEA
120

FOOD FOR THOUGHT